T0150380

LEARNING
AS WE GO

*The Hoover Institution and Education Next Books
gratefully acknowledge the following individuals
and foundations for their support of this research on
education policy and reform.*

LYNDE AND HARRY BRADLEY FOUNDATION

KORET FOUNDATION

EDMUND AND JEANNIK LITTLEFIELD FOUNDATION

BERNARD AND CATHERINE SCHWARTZ FOUNDATION

WILLIAM E. SIMON FOUNDATION

BOYD AND JILL SMITH

TAD AND DIANNE TAUBE FOUNDATION

JACK AND MARY WHEATLEY

THE HOOVER INSTITUTION'S KORET TASK FORCE ON K–12 EDUCATION

LEARNING
AS WE GO

WHY
SCHOOL
CHOICE
IS WORTH
THE WAIT

PAUL T. HILL

EDUCATION
next
B O O K S

HOOVER INSTITUTION PRESS
STANFORD UNIVERSITY
STANFORD, CALIFORNIA

The Hoover Institution on War, Revolution and Peace, founded at Stanford University in 1919 by Herbert Hoover, who went on to become the thirty-first president of the United States, is an interdisciplinary research center for advanced study on domestic and international affairs. The views expressed in its publications are entirely those of the authors and do not necessarily reflect the views of the staff, officers, or Board of Overseers of the Hoover Institution.

www.hoover.org

B O O K S

An imprint of the Hoover Institution Press
Hoover Institution Press Publication No. 577

First printing, 2010
17 16 15 14 13 12 11 10   9 8 7 6 5 4 3 2 1

Manufactured in the United States of America

The paper used in this publication meets the minimum requirements of the American National Standard for Information Sciences— Permanence of Paper for Printed Library Materials, ANSI Z39.48–1992. ∞

Cataloging-in-Publication Data is available from Library of Congress.

ISBN-13: 978-0-8179-1014-3 (hardback : alk. paper)
ISBN-13: 978-0-8179-1013-6 (e-book version)

To Alice, who always wants to know how things work.

CONTENTS

PREFACE

In education policy, the terms of debate are usually badly framed. Reformers claim that a desired action (e.g., higher standards, performance-based pay, or new spending), will lead to better schools all by themselves, even if nothing else changes. That is never true. But opponents of change, often those who stand to lose position or privilege if a proposed measure is adopted, use an equally flawed argument. They claim that since whatever change they are fighting against can't solve every problem, then it should not be tried. Hence, one side claims that a measure is sufficient when, at best, it is necessary, while the other claims that the same measure is not necessary because it is not sufficient.

School choice, the most hotly contested issue in public education, gets such treatment.

The consequences of bad framing became painfully clear to me during a debate staged by my colleagues on the Hoover Institution's Koret Task Force on K–12 Education. The question posed for debate was whether *choice* or *curriculum* was the key to more effective schools. Debaters on both sides had to act as if they did not know the important issues. Those assigned to argue against choice had to forget that the rigorous curriculum, developed by one of them, was used much more often in schools of choice than in district run public schools. Few public school districts could support a curriculum that was as focused and demanded so much work from teachers and students. Those arguing for choice had to act as if they believed choice led directly to better schools, rather than it acting indirectly by giving school leaders the freedom to implement coherent curricula and allowing parents to avoid curricula they dislike and find ones that work for their children. The silliness of the question made for an entertaining debate, but the store of human knowledge did not increase that day.

What the debate made obvious is that the real argument for choice is complex and conditional, not simple. Forces of competition and freedom are real but don't guarantee success every time. Moreover, opponents can block or slow down choice, and opportunists can corrupt it.

Choice programs are embattled in public education, but they exist. Are their successes obvious to the naked eye of any honest observer? No. Instead, these successes are uneven and the results are often so subtle that serious people can debate whether they are real or are instead artifacts of research and analysis techniques.

How then do we understand how choice works when it does, and what slows it down or blocks it? Explaining those subtleties is the business of this book. It arises from years of thinking about choice, playing with causal models, looking at evidence, and arguing with friends.

Acknowledgments

My current and past colleagues in this endeavor on the Hoover Institution's Koret Task Force on K–12 Education, John Chubb, Williamson Evers, Checker Finn, Eric Hanushek, E.D. Hirsch, Caroline Hoxby, Tom Loveless, Terry Moe, Paul Peterson, Diane Ravitch, and Herbert Walberg were critical and influential friends. They didn't write this book, and maybe wouldn't have written anything like it, but they were indispensable to its development.

I also owe debts to long-time collaborators at the Center on Reinventing Public Education, Robin Lake, Dan Goldhaber, Ashley Jochim, Sam Sperry, and James Harvey; to Bruno Manno, Jane Hannaway, Howard Fuller, the late Tom Glennan, Jeff Henig, Dean Millot, and Tony Bryk; and to members of the Brookings Institution commission I led on Doing School Choice Right. All of them, by putting up with my speculations and tracing my flow diagrams, encouraged me to consider choice not as a magic potion but as a normal public policy intervention whose results depend on many things.

Thanks also to the Hoover Institution staff for steady support, particularly director John Raisian, senior associate director Richard Sousa, and associate director Eryn Witcher (communications director). Additionally, I would like to thank copyeditor Barbara Egbert.

Also a big thanks to Center on Reinventing Public Education staffer Deb Britt, who makes sure my writing is at least arguably in English.

CHAPTER 1

INTRODUCTION

Have publicly funded school choice programs—charter schools in forty-three states and vouchers in a few localities—been qualified successes or crashing failures? Only sworn opponents of school choice will argue for failure, but no one can argue that it has been an overwhelming success. Neutrals and choice supporters alike will agree that these initiatives have been qualified successes. Even the most rigorous studies of student achievement in charter and voucher schools find some dramatic successes and many mixed results.

How does this square with the rhetoric of choice supporters who promised much more effective schools and an era of innovation? Predictions of quick and dramatic success for school choice were in part the normal over-promising associated with advocacy. But to my knowledge choice supporters didn't consciously make inflated predictions. Even in secret, choice supporters did not say to one another, "This will take a long time and the early results will be meager but we can't admit that publicly." To the contrary— strong choice supporters were the truest believers.

Is there something wrong with the theories behind the school choice movement? No, indeed. But are the theories valid as generalizations but too simple to predict real events, and much slower to act than choice supporters expected? The answer is yes. The theories behind school choice are valid in the same sense that Newton's basic equations in physics are valid: they identify inexorable forces and fundamental relationships but in doing so they assume idealized conditions that are never perfectly met in the real world. To explain, predict, or control real events one would have to take account of factors the theories assume away, like friction and atmospheric pressure in the case of Newton's laws of motion. The same is true of theories of human or market behavior. This book will consider the real-world factors that can complicate, delay, and even in some instances interfere with the cause-and-effect relationships identified by the theories behind school choice.

The core predictions of choice theorists are true: that allowing parents to choose their children's schools and allowing people with new ideas about instruction to compete for students and public funds will create performance pressures that raise the quality of schools available to everyone. But they are true in the same sense that Newton's predictions that objects fall to earth are true. However, just as the falling of real-world objects can depend on many factors not considered in Newton's original equations (e.g., temperature, air resistance, structures blocking movement), so also the progress of choice in the real world can be complicated.

Questions about complex causality and realistic timing are important for people convinced as I am that choice is a necessary condition for improvement of K–12 education. It is important for school choice supporters to know how choice is likely to work and how long it will take to have its promised effects. In ignorance of these things, and especially expecting choice to work instantly, people who know public education needs to change might nonetheless decide that they must abandon choice in favor of something else. That would not make choice any less inevitable in the long run, but it would delay the full development of choice, to the detriment of children and ultimately our nation's economy.

Feeble results and long delays provide ammunition for defenders of the status quo who fear choice and who hope to roll back any gains made. Increased foundation support for strengthening bureaucracy and standardizing instruction in all schools is an example of perverse reactions. As one prominent foundation head who had invested a lot in choice recently said, "Charter schools are killing me with my board. I have to find something to support that will work quicker." Former choice supporters, including Diane Ravitch, have switched sides, arguing for curriculum standardization, not competition and innovation.

Important choice supporters in foundations, elective office, and academia have been slower to draw conclusions. As Robin J. Lake has shown, state legislators who sponsored charter legislation did not expect dramatic results overnight, and are not driven to action by studies showing mixed results for students.[1] Jeffrey Henig has also shown that anti-choice sentiment among elected officials has not grown appreciably despite widely publicized studies critical of charters.[2]

That said, it is not clear how steadily key elected officials and foundation heads will maintain their support for choice. It would help if choice supporters were much clearer than they have been

1. Robin J. Lake, "The State of Charter Achievement Research," in Julian R. Betts and Paul T. Hill, eds., *Taking Measure of Charter Schools* (Lanham, Md.: Rowman and Littlefield, 2009).

2. Jeffrey Henig, *Spin Cycle: How Research Is Used in Policy Debates: The Case of Charter Schools* (New York: Russell Sage Foundation/The Century Foundation, 2008).

about how choice is likely to work, through what sequences of events and over how long a time. In order to build realistic expectations among supporters whose commitment can't be presumed over the long run, it is also important to know what is likely to get in the way of choice, and what can be done to facilitate its operation.

Figure 1, below, summarizes the "virtuous cycle" of continuous improvement that school choice was supposed to introduce to public education. It depicts the theory behind school choice:

+ Parents will seek the best schools for their children and will therefore withdraw children from schools that are either of low quality or do not match the needs of particular students.

Figure 1: The Virtuous Cycle Stimulated by School Choice

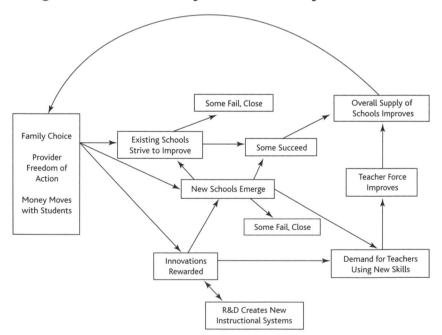

+ New schools will emerge to compete for students on the basis of either quality in some general sense or a match to the distinctive talents and motivations of a particular group of students.
+ Existing schools, forced to compete, will strive to improve their appeal to parents, either by raising quality or by ensuring that their programs are better targeted to match the needs of particular students.
+ Entrepreneurs will try to develop innovative schools that can be highly productive and therefore attractive to parents.
+ Potential innovators will work to meet the demand for new, more productive ways to provide instruction.
+ New and existing schools will pay premiums for teachers who are either extremely productive or have rare skills (e.g., the ability to teach math or science).
+ Talented people who might not have considered teaching will be attracted by prospects for better pay and working conditions.
+ Incumbent teachers will also respond to incentives to upgrade their skills.
+ Together, existing schools' efforts to improve, instructional innovation, and enhancement of the teaching force will improve the overall supply of schools.
+ Once competition starts to work, schools that were initially successful might find students leaving for even better schools, so that the virtuous cycle will be unending, as innovations and new competitors force all schools to continue improving.

This is the same kind of theory that predicts greater innovation, lower prices, and greater customer satisfaction in a competitive market for any good or service, compared to monopoly provision. However, as in other markets, there are time lags and other complexities that can, at a particular time, make it look like the market is not working as predicted. In the 1970s American automakers acted as if they had no competitors except one another and cars got worse, not better. For years they ignored signs that many Americans were switching to Hondas and Toyotas, but when the U.S. companies woke up to the threat they desperately tried to improve their products.

The model sketched in Figure 1 shows that the current debate, about whether improvement of America's schools depends more on choice or curriculum, is based on a false premise. Both choice and changes in instruction are necessary, and they are causally related. Curriculum innovation and other changes in human resources and instructional methods are needed to improve students' instructional experience and ensure better results for the millions of children now in ineffective schools. But choice is needed to create circumstances that let those changes come about. Under our system of politically controlled public education, curriculum is a product of interest group bargaining, innovation is constrained by regulatory controls on use of time and dollars, and human resource pools are constrained by certification rules and labor agreements that protect incumbents.

Choice opens up what our public education system now holds tight, and therefore allows innovations in curriculum and other aspects of instruction that are now not possible. That is why, for example, innovative schooling models like KIPP and E.D. Hirsch's Core Knowledge schools rely so heavily on chartering. Leaders of those schools must have freedoms that school districts and collective bargaining agreements seldom permit. Thus, choice is a necessary if not sufficient condition for needed innovations in curriculum, methods, use of time, and human resources.

In education, the process pictured above has started, though slowly and in isolated places. Some money is moving with children to charter and voucher schools. Enough new charter schools have emerged to serve nearly 4 percent of public school students. Some districts are struggling to improve their schools and replace their weakest ones. In a few notable cases (e.g., the District of Columbia; Dayton, Ohio; and New Orleans) charter schools serve a quarter or more of all students and have forced school districts and even teachers' unions to search for ways to become more competitive.

However, growth of choice is much less evident in the rest of the country. Charter schools are operating in only about 1 in 20 school districts,[3] meaning that the vast majority of U.S. school districts have none. Moreover, most states with laws permitting charter schools have very few: the median number in 2007 was less than forty. Seven of these states had two, one, or zero charter schools.[4]

Choice is growing, but slowly. Under current circumstances its effects—and the likelihood that it will drive the kind of virtuous cycle explained above—are modest. No doubt the numbers of charter schools will continue to grow incrementally. But under current laws and at the current level of investment and effort, it is not clear when if ever choice will reach its full potential.

Most of the following discussion focuses on charter schools—independently run schools that operate under performance contracts with government agencies and receive government funding on an agreed rate for every child they enroll—because they are

3. A consensus estimate of people who track charter school growth at the National Charter School Research Project and the National Alliance for Public Charter Schools.

4. Jon Christensen and Robin J. Lake, "The National Charter School Landscape in 2007," in Robin J. Lake, ed., *Hopes, Fears, & Reality: A Balanced Look at American Charter Schools in 2007*, Seattle, National Charter School Research Project, 2007, p 3.

the most numerous publicly funded schools of choice. Vouchers—government funds to pay tuition in any school parents choose—entail less governmental oversight and thus support purer forms of choice. However, vouchers are now limited to a few big cities with large numbers of available parochial schools, and to a few state programs that provide only a fraction of the cost of enrolling a student. Though voucher programs have produced important local benefits, they have not sparked a significant supply response of new schools, teachers, or changes in district-run schools. This is due in part to the fact that voucher programs provide lower per-pupil subsidies than do state charter laws, making chartering the more workable mechanism for anyone wanting to start a new publicly funded school.

Though different voucher designs (covering more students and paying full tuition in private schools) could fuel the virtuous cycle, today's voucher programs have much more limited effects than the much larger and better-funded charter school initiatives.

Charter schools offer some benefits regular public schools don't, especially safer environments for children in inner-city neighborhoods and grade configurations (e.g., K–8 and K–12) that parents want but districts are not well organized to provide. In some localities, hundreds of individuals from elite schools, who previously chose other professions, are agreeing to teach in schools of choice.

However, these effects do not amount to full operation of the virtuous cycle. The average quality of new schools is not uniformly high, and existing schools can often hold onto their students without making significant changes. The predicted technical innovations and labor force transformation have not yet occurred.

The effects cited above are also limited to a few localities in which district-run public schools are in disastrous shape. The new schools offered are not particularly innovative and are attractive only in comparison to very bad available options. New instructional methods and uses of technology are too expensive to develop on charter schools' slender budgets, and existing charter schools can draw students by providing more caring environments, not by teaching differently. Where charter schools have made the greatest inroads they also rely heavily on very shallow pools of human resources—Teach For America alumni, veteran public school teachers who are maxed out on their government pensions and who want a new challenge, people who have made their fortunes in business or engineering and want to give something back to the community. Such people are tremendous assets to charter schools, but their numbers—and the numbers of charter schools that can rely on them—are strictly limited.

These facts point to serious constraints on the numbers and competitiveness of charter schools. Charter schools now appeal to parents and teachers who are grossly unhappy with conventional public schools, because of a lack of safety or inattention to individual students' needs.[5] Public school parents whose children are reasonably safe and are learning at a moderate rate, or teachers who have made their peace with an annoying but reliable employer, have little reason to switch. Thus, charter schools are more a safety valve for parents and teachers who can't find a comfortable place in public schools than a superior product that everyone wants.

Why haven't schools of choice yet achieved a broader appeal? Four factors explain the delay. The first and most important factor is political opposition. Choice creates benefits for families, students, and educators who have new ideas about effective instruction, but it also breaks monopolies and puts institutions (e.g., traditional school districts) and jobs at risk. It also generates opposition from people

5. Paul Teske, Jody Fitzpatrick and Gabriel Kaplan, *Opening Doors: How Low-Income Parents Search for the Right School* (Seattle, WA: Center on Reinventing Public Education, University of Washington, 2007).

who believe that governmental control is the only way to promote social justice. As the next chapter will show, opposition to choice does not go away easily; it takes time to create new coalitions in support of choice and weaken the coalitions that oppose it.

The second factor is composed of policies and regulations—themselves the results of politics that favor incumbent administrators, educators, and interest groups—that either create big obstacles to the success of school choice or go only halfway toward creating the conditions necessary for its full operation. Halfway provisions include voucher and charter programs that provide only fractions of the amounts of money necessary to support a school, and provisions that make it difficult for students and teachers to transfer to schools of choice. Obstacles include caps on the numbers of charter schools and laws that let school boards decide whether to allow charter schools to compete in their jurisdictions.

Third is an entrenched system built on procedure, compliance, employee protection, and secrecy about resource use and productivity. The habit of living inside such a system makes it very difficult for parents and educators to imagine working differently even when there are opportunities to do so. As Westerners learned when they tried to introduce capitalism and democracy to the former Soviet Union, building a system of choice on top of one based on regulation is a very different problem than creating choice from the ground up. As in Russia, efforts to introduce transparency, performance accountability, and personal initiative clash with habits of secrecy, lack of accountability, and passivity. Naïve market-based initiatives often encounter unexpected problems and produce meager results.[6]

6. On the problems of private organizations entering fields previously dominated by government see Rick Geddes, *Competing with the Government: Anticompetitive Behavior and Public Enterprises* (Stanford: Hoover Press, 2004).

A fourth source of delays is a set of time lags intrinsic to the operation of a system of choice. It takes time for educators to learn how to operate effectively in new competitive environments and for new school providers to learn how to provide effective schools. It takes time to develop, test, and refine instructional systems that make new uses of technology and student and teacher work, and to develop approaches to instruction that are more effective but cost no more than conventional public schools. It takes time to build a pipeline of people who know what it means to run a school in a competitive environment, and to figure out how to operate stable schools with non-traditional teachers who have many skills and can move rapidly between education and other careers.

Even if politics, policy, and regulation were less hostile to school choice, the necessary process of dismantling a strongly defended system and building knowledge, capacity, and human resources would take a significant amount of time. Choice supporters need to acknowledge that positive results will not just come automatically, and full development of the virtuous cycle will take time. To reach its potential in education, choice will need steady, persistent support based on an understanding of what it will take, not doctrinaire insistence that analysis and strategic investment are counterproductive because the market will automatically provide whatever is needed.

It will be harder to get dramatic results from school choice, and the actions that must be taken will be more difficult, than some supporters had hoped. It is now clear that schools of choice:

Are hard to run. Principals from district-run schools are often not ready to make the financing, hiring, firing, admissions, and self-assessment decisions that fall on them. Some learn but others don't. Those who take the "my way or the highway" attitude celebrated in district-run schools come into conflict with school founders, parents, and those who had definite reasons for choosing the school.

Are demanding places to teach and aren't for everybody. Teachers become partners in an enterprise that must sink or swim depending on performance. Hours, assignments, pay, and job security can't be guaranteed by a deep-pocket school district, but are products of collaborative effort at the school level. Many former public school teachers find that schools of choice don't offer the security and bounded responsibility that made the profession attractive in the first place.

Can't compete successfully with district-run public schools unless they get as much money for pupils they educate. Early hopes that choice would lead to schools that were both cheaper and better ignored the fact that schools of choice must compete for teachers and instructional materials in markets where the prices are set by school districts.

Need to prove themselves on the same tests and other outcome measures as other schools. Early hopes that charter and voucher schools would be so obviously great that no fine outcome measures would be needed have been dashed. So have hopes that families and communities would be willing to wait until children had completed school to make judgments about school performance.

Are hard to reproduce, even when particular schools are successful and well known. Innovative schools like San Diego's High Tech High can struggle to spin off even one good clone.

Organizations trying to run many schools of choice struggle with costs and quality and can reproduce inefficient school district central offices.

Hindsight makes these conclusions obvious. But together they mean that schools of choice have a tougher time than expected finding leaders and teachers, getting the funds they need to be run effectively, proving that their programs work, and creating stable parent clienteles. Though charter and voucher schools have been far less obviously superior than some of their supporters had hoped, there is some evidence that schools of choice are getting more effective[7] and school providers are getting better at starting and running schools. Recent charter school studies have been more likely to find positive student achievement results, and new schools associated with for- and non-profit management organizations appear to work well more quickly than isolated one-off schools. But these results are more positive tendencies than definitive evidence that would sway a skeptical audience.

This book examines the factors that complicate and delay establishment of the virtuous cycle pictured in Figure 1. It hopes to set off a discussion leading to more realistic expectations about timing and a more complete understanding of what must be done to make choice work.

Chapter 2, following this introduction, examines the politics of choice. It shows how groups whose advantages are threatened by the growth of public school choice work to impede its progress, and how groups that favor choice or stand to benefit from

7. Julian R. Betts and Emily Tang, "Value-Added and Experimental Studies of the Effect of Charter Schools on Student Achievement: A Literature Review," in Robin J. Lake, *Hopes, Fears, & Reality: A Balanced Look at American Charter Schools in 2008*, Seattle, National Charter School Research Project, 2008.

it—including those concerned about the welfare of students whom the public schools now serve poorly—work to advance it. This process—slow expansion of the constituency for choice and gradual splintering of formerly dominant coalitions opposed to it—is the first of many connected pro-choice processes that have their own natural rhythm and inevitably take a lot of time.

Chapters 3 through 7 focus on five key elements of the virtuous cycle: the links between flows of money and pressure on existing schools to improve; the challenges of increasing the number of high-performing schools of choice; innovation in instruction and school operation to make new schools more productive and therefore give them a competitive edge that will drive others to imitate them; improvement of the teaching force; and closures of bad schools. Each section discusses the existing causes of slow progress. Chapter 8 then suggests changes in public policy and philanthropic investment that could overcome barriers and increase the rate of progress toward full operation of the virtuous cycle.

The book as a whole makes two points I did not anticipate making when I started writing it. The first is that choice is likely to have more an evolutionary than a revolutionary effect on K–12 public education. For all the events sketched on Figure 1 to occur, and for them to affect enough localities that American public education is transformed, is likely to take decades, as new ideas about instruction are developed and tested, growing numbers of parents see the advantages of more innovative schools, and whole cohorts of people who expect to work in new ways replace teachers, principals, and administrators who were trained to work in bureaucracies.

The second point is that the full effects of choice will come much more quickly through a combination of external competition and deliberate re-engineering of existing public school systems than through competition alone. Though it is necessary that schools of choice increase in number and continue to draw students and money out of school districts, these processes will work at a glacial pace as long as school districts are able to gain unconditional public subsidies, shift funds from students whose parents are undemanding to children of aggressive parents, and offer teachers pay and benefit packages buttressed by hidden taxpayer subsidies. These arrangements, which buffer districts from the effects of competition, must be removed expressly through state legislative actions that force districts to operate transparently and within real spending constraints. Efforts to transform districts from vertically integrated bureaucracies into managers of portfolios of schools funded equitably but operated by many different providers, evident today in big cities like New York, Chicago, New Orleans, Denver, and Hartford, Connecticut, are indispensable for the development of a virtuous cycle.[8]

Choice supporters are wrong if they think that strategic investment, analysis, and problem solving, including efforts to improve state education agencies and school districts, are likely only to get in the way of market forces. To the contrary, without a nuanced and multi-sector strategy, school choice might not, at least in our lifetimes, produce all the benefits we hope for.

8. On the evolution of portfolio-based school districts see Paul T. Hill, Christine Campbell, David Menefee-Libey, Brianna Dusseault, Michael DeArmond, and Betheny Gross, *Portfolio School Districts for Big Cities: An Interim Report* (Seattle,WA: Center on Reinventing Public Education, University of Washington, 2009).

CHAPTER 2

THE SLOW BUT STEADY
PROGRESS OF
PRO-CHOICE POLITICS

Legendary political scientist E.E. Schattschneider drew a vivid analogy between politics and a tussle between two individuals in a public street.[1] As he observed, the outcome depends less on the relative strength of the initial combatants than on the behavior of the crowd. The weaker of the two can win by attracting support from others. If the initially weaker party gains the upper hand, the other party must either seek support or accept defeat. Parties other than the original combatants respond for their own reasons, whether they join one side or stay aloof.

This simple observation explains a great deal about the politics of choice.[2] Our national deliberation about school choice features philosophical debates, invention and litigation of new legal principles, emotional calls to loyalty and revolution, and disputes

---

1. E.E. Schattschneider, *The Semisovereign People: A Realist's View of Democracy in America* (New York: Holt, Rinehart, & Winston, 1960).

2. For a greatly expanded version of this argument see Paul T. Hill and Ashley E. Jochim, "Political Perspectives on School Choice," in Mark Berends, Matthew Springer, Dale Ballou, and Herbert Walberg, eds., *Handbook of Research on School Choice* (New York: Routledge, 2009), pp. 1-18.

about social science findings. But not to see the unity of all of these actions as elements of a larger political struggle is to miss their real significance.

Today, the vast preponderance of governmental money appropriated for education is spent by local school districts. Federal and state laws constrain some spending and set some basic requirements (e.g., for courses to be taught, teacher qualifications, and numbers of days that schools must be open). Subject only to those constraints, districts own and operate schools, determine what instructional and other programs schools will offer, determine how children are assigned to schools, directly employ and assign teachers and principals, provide advice and assistance to schools, and keep whatever data are required to assess school performance. Districts, not individual schools or students, are the lowest level to which funds can be unambiguously traced; schools are not cost centers and they receive resources the district purchases and prices according to district policy, not market values.

The school system is a reliable employer and a stable provider of benefits to schools and neighborhoods whose leaders know how to influence school board and central office decision-making. This system is hard to understand and hard to change. A combination of private and governmental interest groups has dominated conventional education policy, and its core strategy is to ensure that the agenda, and the set of groups whose demands are seriously considered, change as little as possible. As Schattschneider would have predicted, groups on the inside—teachers' unions, state and local school system employees, organized parent groups, and schools of education—maintain control by reducing the visibility of current arrangements and resisting changes to policy.

Until recently, parents who wanted alternatives to their district schools had no options other than private schools—and paying private school tuition. Educators who had new ideas about how to run schools could not get permission or access to the funds needed to try them out. School districts and schools of education controlled access to jobs in education. School choice challenges these uses of governmental funds and power in K–12 education.

Beginning in the 1970s, faced with urban public schools' continuing inability to offer effective instruction for poor and disadvantaged children, a number of interest groups began pressing for change. Some groups tried to move the system from within, via standards-based reform and alignment of polities, without threatening key interest groups or forcing major reallocations of money. Others, convinced marginal changes would not be effective, agitated for more fundamental changes in control of money, control of schools, and opportunities for students. These groups, which I shall loosely call the choice movement, included many actors (scholars, foundations, politicians, interest groups) that previously had little to do with education policy. Established groups challenged the new entrants' legitimacy and ridiculed their ideas, but the new groups elaborated their agendas and gained allies.

Today, a protracted conflict over school choice is being fought on many issues and at every level of government. Proposals for school choice set off conflict in almost every level of government and educational administration. Choice reduces the scope of unchecked action by some parties—particularly incumbent district leaders and teacher union heads—and expands the options of others, including private groups that want to run publicly funded schools and parents who want something different for their children. Choice can affect broader interests, including elected officials who want to maintain the organizational strength of public employee unions, companies that would like to create national chains of charter schools, and philanthropies on the left and right.

Choice can also become political at the grass roots, when individuals who are happy with their current schools fear they will be weakened by losses of students to charter or private schools, and when parents who choose new options come under attack.

As Schattschneider would have predicted, the issues keep evolving. Outsider groups seek new leverage and allies; some insider groups defect and join the outsiders; and insiders both attack their challengers and make compromises to hold their coalition together. Today, battles about school choice are being fought:

- *In state legislatures* over statewide voucher plans, vouchers targeted for handicapped students, home schooling and cyber-schooling policies, charter school laws, tuition tax credits, collective bargaining laws, and alternative routes into teaching;
- *In state departments of education* over charter school policy, alternative teacher certification, accountability for schools of choice, and use of state takeover powers to force reallocation of funds and increased use of chartering and school contracting in troubled urban districts;
- *In Congress* over vouchers in the District of Columbia, assistance to charter schools, No Child Left Behind (NCLB) provisions requiring new options for children in consistently low performing schools, and tuition tax credits;
- *In school districts* over whether to charter schools and hire school contractors, accountability for schools of choice, responsibility for informing parents about options, how to cope with loss of funding when families opt for schools of choice, and how to develop new sources of principals and teachers;
- *In the forum of public opinion*, over whether choice will destroy or strengthen public education, whether schools of choice

help or harm children, and whether conservative groups in the choice coalition have a legitimate place in a polity debate.

Clearly, the scope of conflict has expanded and is likely to continue doing so. Choice proponents are trying to expand the scope of conflict in order to introduce or strengthen charters, vouchers, and other forms of choice, and defenders of the still-dominant traditional approaches and institutions are defending their positions.

Interests on the Contending Sides

The defensive (anti-choice) side. School choice threatens to upset existing patterns of resource allocation and substantive decision-making. It is too simple to say that the interests standing against choice are those that now benefit most from the existing arrangements in public education—but only a little. There are individuals and groups with no children in schools and no personal financial interests at stake who nonetheless adhere to the ideas sketched above. Moreover, some families that could exercise choices that might benefit their children educationally avoid doing so, out of a belief that keeping their children in traditional public schools is an act of civic virtue.

However, the main interests at stake are those of people whose jobs, incomes, or positions of power depend on the current arrangements in public education. These groups include current public school employees, particularly permanent district central office staff, state school officials, and teachers' unions.

These groups have strong interests in keeping key decisions within traditional channels. Most choice plans eliminate automatic spending on state and district bureaucracies, requiring instead that funds flow first to the schools parents choose and then to external service providers only if schools decide to buy their services. These provisions threaten bureaucracies that now control as much as half the money available for public education and offer guaranteed life-time employment to their staffs. Most choice plans also transfer authority for teacher-hiring and pay-setting to individual schools. This further weakens the central bureaucracies that are now staffed to hire and allocate teachers. More importantly, it under-cuts teachers' unions in two ways. By making individual schools the employers of teachers, choice would render district-wide collec-tive bargaining units moot: teachers would organize at the school rather than district level. Teachers' unions would therefore lose the capacity to control teacher pay and working conditions for a whole district with one collective bargaining agreement. They would also be at risk of losing members as teachers in some schools might choose not to unionize, or to affiliate with unions other than the American Federation of Teachers (AFT) and National Education Association (NEA).

Interests associated with the education of children with dis-abilities have a particularly complicated history with choice. As the one group with enormous leverage to obtain the services they need from the traditional public schools, parents of disabled chil-dren kept their distance from choice in the 1980s and early 1990s. School district special education specialists and groups advocat-ing for disabled children also expressed strong skepticism. The fact that most choice programs called for transparent alloca-tion of funds on a per-pupil basis also threatened to reduce fund-ing for district special education bureaus and portended political problems, as relatively high levels of spending on disabled chil-dren became more visible. In general, these groups preferred not to widen the scope of policymaking any further. However, char-ter schools split the special education parent community, as some parents chose charter schools to escape "handicapped" labels that had been–or might be–attached to their children. Many of these parents were attracted to charter elementary schools that pledged to intervene early in order to prevent development of learning deficits that might lead children to be classified as disabled. To date, enough parents are satisfied with charter schools to maintain this split in the special education community.

Expanding the scope of conflict to include new independent school providers, and to allow parents to take public funds when they transfer their children to schools not run by local districts, takes money and control away from district and state employees' and teachers' unions. These groups therefore constitute a determined anti-choice coalition. Unions have dedicated significant resources to defeating choice proposals in both the legislative and initiative processes. In California, for example, the California Teachers Association outspent proponents of a voucher plan by ten to one, spending $13 million to defeat the initiative.[3]

Other groups join the coalition, more because of the ways they choose to define their interests than because choice unambiguously reduces their income or power. School boards, whose functions would be eliminated by voucher plans but potentially strengthened by laws that allow them to oversee charter schools, almost invariably oppose all forms of choice. Though they struggle against unions and district bureaucracies for control of schools, school boards are nonetheless afraid that contracts with independent school providers would give them even less leverage than they now have. The national Parent Teacher Association (PTA) and some chapters of the League of Women Voters, whose institutional

3. R.C. Bulman and D.L. Kirp, "The Shifting Politics of School Choice," in S.D. Sugarman and F.R. Kemerer, eds., *School Choice and Social Controversy: Politics, Policy, and Law* (Washington, D.C.: Brookings Institution Press, 1999).

interests could arguably be enhanced by increasing families' schooling options, nonetheless consistently oppose voucher programs.
These groups might be acting out of fear of the unknown, but they
might also be motivated simply by solidarity with their old allies in
school districts and teachers' unions.

The traditional civil rights coalition of activist law firms, the
ACLU, groups like the NAACP, and the main industrial unions have
generally opposed choice plans. This posture might reflect a desire
to retain solidarity with teachers' unions, but it also reflects fears
that choice could further isolate and harm low-income and minority (particularly black) children. In recent years the civil rights coalition against choice has been weakened by defections from groups
that think traditional public schools have served the disadvantaged
so badly that other alternatives are necessary. Both the National
Council of La Raza and the Citizens' Commission on Civil Rights,
for example, support charter schools. As the concluding section will
show, choice is proving to be a wedge issue splitting the civil rights
movement, the business community, and both political parties.

The core strategy of choice opponents is to keep control of
money and decisions in the hands of elected officials and public
employees at the local, state, and federal levels; to avoid increasing
parents' ability to allocate taxpayer money by their choices; and to
prevent independent providers from receiving public funds.

Choice opponents defend the existing roles and powers of
school boards, school district central offices, state boards of education, state and local units charged to administer federal categorical
programs like Title I, state units that define teacher certification
rules, and teachers' unions. These groups contend with one another
every day over many issues, but faced with the threat that new entities might seize control of funds and decision-making, they prefer
the existing arrangements.

THE SLOW BUT STEADY PROGRESS   25

These institutions are also eager to keep legislative decision-making in familiar committees and subcommittees, where elected members and staff also have positions to defend. On occasion, newly elected legislators get assigned to education authorization and appropriations committees, changing the balance of power enough to make the committees friendlier to choice (as happened in Congress to enable passage of the District of Columbia voucher bill). The traditional education committees' powers are also under challenge by other legislators more open to choice, particularly members of appropriations subcommittees that can fund schools of choice via tax measures like tuition credits and special vouchers for children with disabilities.

Finally, groups hoping to keep decision-making within familiar channels on occasion appeal to courts, asking them to defend traditional administrative mechanisms and the principle of local control against charter and voucher proposals. Though the results of these efforts have varied (rulings in favor of vouchers and charters in Ohio and Wisconsin, rulings against vouchers and for school board control in Colorado and Florida), it seems likely that defenders of the existing arrangements will continue looking for friendly courts.

The expansive (pro-choice) side. Outsiders struggle to widen the scope of conflict and bring new participants into the political process by mobilizing the public or shifting the debate to friendlier venues.[4] These "outside initiators" exert pressure on the subsystem, as those in power resist these efforts. On the pro-choice side three types of interest groups are active. Some are motivated by ideology, others by desire to use public funds in ways that benefit businesses and private schools, and still others by a desire to advance

4. F.R. Baumgartner and B.D. Jones, *Agendas and Instability in American Politics* (Chicago: University of Chicago Press, 1993).

civic objectives. Though these groups are distinct in membership and objectives, together they helped move discussions of school choice into the arena of public opinion.[5]

When Milton Friedman articulated the first voucher proposal in 1955, his supporters fell squarely in the ideological category. These fervent believers in free market solutions ran a campaign for choice as pure as any. Public policy think tanks, conservative and libertarian political parties, and economists have generally supported a variety of choice plans, including vouchers, public school choice, and charters. These groups form the ideological base of the choice movement.

Despite their intense commitment to school choice, these organizations are generally not effective in mobilizing broader support for choice. To many, they came across as extremists, "right-wing" crusaders who would do anything to shrink the capacity of government. If the choice coalition stopped here, little political progress could be made.

As education drew an increasing amount of attention from state and federal policymakers, the number of actors working in favor of choice expanded. Business organizations and supporters of religious schools became increasingly active in education politics. These "private interests," which have a direct stake in the enactment of choice policies, include businesses interested in operating schools and in providing alternative teacher programs and other educational services, and private religious schools seeking access to public funding.

At the same time, many traditional stakeholders in education, such as urban civic organizations, civil rights groups, and philanthropic foundations, expressed impatience with the perceived

5. T.L. Mazzoni, "Analyzing State School Policymaking: An Arena Model," *Educational Evaluation and Policy Analysis*, 12(2), 1991, pp. 115-138.

difficulties in transforming traditional public schools, especially those serving low-income students in cities. In the face of declining or stagnant academic achievement, particularly in urban school districts, these civic organizations actively supported choice proposals. La Raza, the Black Alliance for Educational Options, and the Citizens' Commission on Civil Rights, all members of the Democratic Party coalition, emerged as civic-motivated supporters of school choice. Moreover, the Democratic Leadership Council (DLC), an admirer of President Bill Clinton's and British Prime Minister Tony Blair's "Third Way" theories of private-public partnerships, took a strong position in favor of charter schools, though not vouchers.

Many of these groups are new to the politics of education, but a handful (e.g., former DLC leaders Andrew Rotherham and Will Marshall) were participants in the inner circles of policymaking. These groups seek access to the educational agenda; they want the power to influence decision-making; and they pursue these goals by expanding the scope of conflict. Rather than relying on traditional decision-making bodies such as local school boards, these interest groups are enlisting the support of governors and presidents, taking their issues to court, and appealing to legislative committees other than those that have traditionally dominated education policy.

As Baumgartner and Jones suggest, by shifting debate to alternative venues, interest groups and policy entrepreneurs may find more receptive audiences for their ideas. Thus, while an institution like a legislative committee may seemingly control an issue like education, its power can be transient, dependent upon the dynamics of the political process. Over the last three decades, the number of institutions involved in education policy has increased rapidly. Local institutions remain in control of a vast array of policy decisions, but federal and state policymakers have increasingly constrained their actions. Furthermore, the executive branch at all three levels of government has taken on new leadership in education, with mayors leading urban school districts, and governors and presidents sponsoring reform legislation. All of this activity suggests a successful campaign on the part of outsiders to expand the scope and number of institutions engaged in education policy.

Initial experiments with choice relied on the goodwill of a handful of state leaders facing significant educational problems. These early choice experiments were limited in their impact on the larger policy debate. However, they did act as demonstration programs and provided "fuel to the fire" at the state level.[6] Supporters of choice, frustrated with attempts to reform through a traditional education subsystem dominated by teachers' unions, school boards, and local school bureaucracies, took their proposals to the state level. In 1987, Minnesota became the first state to pass an open enrollment plan, allowing students to attend public schools anywhere in the state regardless of residential location, and in 1991 it passed the nation's first charter school law.

The 1980s were a time of increasing turmoil in public education. The National Commission on Excellence in Education's report, *A Nation at Risk*, was released in 1983, fueling concerns regarding American economic competitiveness. At the same time, ideological allies of choice such as Ronald Reagan were elected to office and provided receptive audiences for proponents of choice at the highest levels of government. Twice Congress considered and rejected a federal voucher program; yet this event represented more of a success than a failure for the voucher movement. The very fact that these groups could get into the agenda in Congress

6. Michael Mintrom, *Policy Entrepreneurs and School Choice* (Washington, D.C.: Georgetown University Press, 2000).

demonstrates the increasing power of choice and the decline of a stable institutional arrangement in education.

While state and federal policymakers have successfully intervened in education, thus expanding opportunities for choice, proponents of "local control" fight to maintain what is left of their political power over education. Similarly, some interest groups decry the increasing executive influence, arguing that mayors are unfit to make decisions on education. In the next section, we consider the flip side of the analysis presented here, that is, the ideas, interests, and institutions that defend the current governing system and limit the scope of conflict in education.

Slow Expansion of the Pro-Choice Side

Max Weber characterized politics as the strong and slow boring of hard boards. This metaphor surely characterizes the politics of choice. To push it a step further, the boring of hard boards gradually creates shavings. Examining the shavings—the splits within pre-existing groups or the defections from pro- and anti-choice coalitions—reveals how the politics of choice have changed over time. Many groups and alliances are now split—or in the process of splitting—over choice:

- *Civil rights groups*, as discussed above, have seen defections to the charter part of the pro-choice side.
- *Black American groups* have growing pro-choice minorities, including the Urban League and NAACP. The Black Alliance for Educational Options (BAEO) is an important pro-choice group with a growing membership.
- *Business groups*, including peak organizations like the Business Roundtable, are now split on choice. Moreover, as support for

choice grows among some business groups it declines among others. For example, business leaders who hoped charter schools would perform better at less cost are disappointed that charter school leaders are now saying they can't run successful schools unless they have as much money as traditional public schools, with whom they have to compete for teachers and other assets.

+ *Unions*, notably the Service Employees International Union, have broken solidarity to endorse charter schools. Small pro-charter factions have also emerged in the teachers' unions. Some charter school managers (prominently Los Angeles-based Green Dot) have invited unions to organize their teachers.

+ *Jewish groups*, once solidly in favor of traditional public school arrangements, have splintered as enrollments in Jewish day schools have increased and more parents see the need for voucher-based tuition assistance.

+ *The Democratic Party*, whose most recent president favored charter schools, retains a solid majority aligned with traditional public school interests. Pro-choice elements of the party include the Democratic Leadership Council and the Center for American Progress, both of which are pro-charter but anti-voucher.

Splitting and re-combining of groups is likely to continue as the choice debate continues. Parents' and teachers' experiences with charter schools and voucher programs, positive or negative, will affect grass-roots opinions. Massive closures of charter school chains, as happened in California in late summer 2005, causing parents to scramble for school placements (Rotherham, 2005), could weaken support for local versions of choice. On the other hand, continued success in providing safer, more personalized, and more orderly schools will build grass-roots support for choice, especially if charter high schools prove to be places parents want to send their children. Of course, grass-roots support for choice could be weakened if school districts find ways to improve their centrally run schools.

Grass-roots support (or indifference) for choice is likely to affect the views of elected officials and the relative strength of interest groups, which are then likely to change their strategies. Pro-charter school groups are already working hard to solve problems evident in early charter schools, motivated in part by the belief that support of elected officials is at stake. Some big city teachers' unions (most notably New York's United Federation of Teachers and the Boston Teachers Union) have been forced by parent and teacher opinion to moderate their opposition to charter schools. Grass-roots sentiment is affected more by local experience and word of mouth than by formal research. But research could ultimately affect state and national politics. Studies on student learning and other outcomes (e.g., graduation rates) in schools of choice will also ultimately strengthen or weaken some groups and could cause realignments. Early findings on voucher programs certainly made choice a salient issue and emboldened supporters. Such results, and both positive and negative studies on charter schools, are regularly attacked as inadequate and politically motivated. Though studies now mainly strengthen the contending sides, more definite findings could change the views of elected officials and foundation leaders.

Conclusion

The political conflict over school choice is in its early days, and it is not likely to end soon with a sweeping victory for either side. The pro-choice side can be expected to continue expanding the scope of conflict to different states and localities and to new forums. Increasing numbers of mayors have made choice part of their rationales for taking over school districts (Chicago, New York, Washington, D.C.) or, in the case of former Indianapolis Mayor Bart Peterson, chartering schools themselves. Talk of litigating school choice as a fundamental right has been growing in some circles. Given the U.S. legal system's openness to novel arguments and new plaintiffs, it would not be surprising to see urban African Americans or recent immigrant groups getting a serious hearing on the claim for such a right. Similarly, the choice movement could easily be expanded to include large and very well organized groups of home-schoolers.

Choice appears likely to spread, but gradually. To a degree, differences between the pro- and anti-choice sides might blur as school districts compete with charters and home schooling by offering alternatives and reallocating their funds so their schools can adapt to student needs. Unions will also accommodate new modes of teacher employment and in some cases even the creation of school-level collective bargaining units and contracts tailored to individual schools. Pure voucher plans, under which school district bureaucracies and teacher unions live and die on whether schools want to patronize them, will probably remain highly contested, with the advantage to opponents. But the politics of choice will probably continue to favor hybrid forms of choice with some regulation and public oversight.

The struggle has become close enough that the formerly dominant opponents of choice have been forced at times to switch strategy from limiting to expanding the conflict. For example, choice opponents in the state of Washington broadened the scope of conflict by running a successful referendum campaign to overturn a charter law passed by the legislature. Utah opponents of a voucher law sponsored a similar public referendum.

Both sides also try to move decisions into the courts whenever the other side wins in normal legislative processes. Moreover, the courts themselves have become political actors at times. State court decisions in charter and voucher litigation are often predictable based on the partisan composition of the court involved (see, for example, the decisions regarding voucher programs in Ohio, Florida, and Colorado).

CHAPTER 3

TOO LITTLE MONEY MOVES WITH STUDENTS

Money is the mother's milk of education, just as of politics. In the virtuous cycle model presented above, students get choice because public money moves with them to whatever school their parents choose. Though all aspects of the virtuous cycle depend on the flow of money, Figure 2 below highlights those processes that are most strongly affected by it.

Any constraints on movement of funds (e.g., on the amounts that can be transferred, on which schools can be chosen) limit the possible benefits to children, the numbers and quality of new schools that are likely to emerge to compete for students, the pressure on school districts to improve their offerings, and the opportunities for changes in who teaches and how teachers work.

This is not to say that the choice movement is only about the money; people who favor dramatic expansions of choice think it will improve education. Claims that school choice is only about money (e.g., business critic Alex Molnar's assertion that charters and vouchers are simply devices for increasing businesses' access to public funds) are political rhetoric, not descriptions of the choice movement.

Figure 2

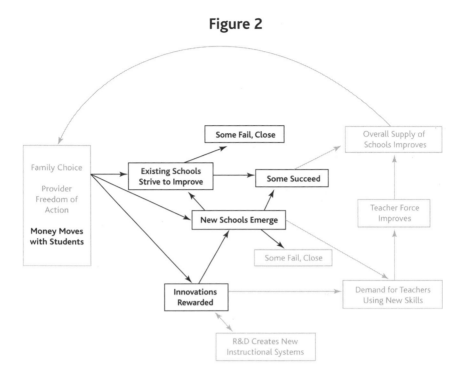

Nonetheless, it is true that choice can't work to its full potential if money does not move. Early choice advocates who claimed that vouchers or charter schools could do better with less money than district-run public schools were also engaging in ungrounded political rhetoric. Enough money must move both to make it possible for new school providers to offer sound instructional programs and to make it necessary for district-run schools to feel the pressure of competition.

Too Little Money for New Schools

In most states, children transferring to charter schools force a movement of only part of the money that district-run schools had received to educate the same children. These amounts differ from state to state, but seldom exceed 90 percent of the per-pupil funding provided to school districts. Most state laws also let school districts keep any funds raised from locally raised taxes or levies, and spend those only on the schools they run directly. Thus, a district that raises 25 percent of its operating expenses locally can continue spending those funds on its own schools, even as students leave for schools of choice. Charter schools therefore often receive as little as 65 percent of the amount available to run regular public schools.

Limits on the flow of money tilt the playing field and therefore dampen the formation of new schools of choice. The only entities that can hope to compete are those that believe they can run effective schools with less money than district-run schools, or that are able to gain some forms of subsidy, such as philanthropic contributions or donated labor. The number of such entities is surely lower than the number of entities that would be interested in running schools if they could expect to recover all the same costs for which their competitors are reimbursed.

Though charter schools get less money than the district-run schools with which they must compete, they must still pay all operating costs and salaries—in markets where prices for key assets like teachers are set by their competitors—and also pay for things that district-run schools get free. In all states but California and the District of Columbia, charter schools must rent or buy facilities from the amounts they get for operating costs, while district-run schools operate rent-free, with facilities costs paid out of district capital accounts. Charter schools must also pay for teacher benefits and retirement out of operating costs, while district schools pay for these out of separate accounts and often, as in Illinois, transfer benefit payments and pension liabilities to the state treasury.

Private schools participating in voucher plans also face major financial disadvantages. Most government-funded vouchers provide less than half the local public school per-pupil expenditure. Even the largest voucher ($7,500 per pupil in the District of Columbia) is more than $10,000 short of the D.C. school district's per-pupil expenditure. Private schools are paid their posted tuition amounts, which are usually far less than $7,500. Because private schools have kept tuition below full costs via separate fundraising and donations from churches, many lose money on every voucher student admitted.

As we shall see in a subsequent section, schools paid in these ways try to compete by hiring cheaper teachers and economizing in other ways. However, charter schools are finding that the number of able people who can work for a long time at below-market wages is strictly limited, and that deferred spending ultimately catches up with them.

Too Little Money to Force Competitive Response

Though charter and voucher programs provide public funding when children move to schools of choice, money usually does not move in the ways most likely to force existing schools to make competitive responses. Instead, existing schools are often shielded from at least some of the consequences of money movement. Thus, a key response to choice—improvement efforts by existing schools—is weaker than predicted.

By this method many districts have experienced increases in their average per-pupil spending levels even as their enrollment and absolute spending levels declined.

Some states (e.g., Massachusetts) also protect public schools against the shock of losing money when students transfer to charters by letting them keep the money for departed students for several years.

The theory outlined in Figure 1 did not consider two additional ways districts could be insulated from the movement of money as families choose.

First, many districts gain compensating increases in their incomes despite student departures for schools of choice. Districts experiencing rapid population growth can gain more students due to in-migration than they lose to choice. These districts—generally in Sunbelt cities that are growing rapidly—do not need to reduce their spending at all, and can avoid any painful reductions in their teaching forces or closure of buildings. Transfers to charter or voucher-funded schools can benefit those districts by reducing overflows and relieving them of the need to build new facilities. Thus, even when money moves with children, schools in such localities have little or no need to improve performance in order to hold onto students.

Second, many—as in worst-case Michigan, with nearly one in five—students who transfer to charter and voucher schools come not from district-run public schools but from fee-charging parochial schools.[1] Parents who paid for parochial schools because of their personalization and safety rather than for their religious affiliations can find charter schools an acceptable, and less expensive, alternative. In big cities with large parochial school establishments, a significant part of charter enrollment can be made up of children whose families had left the public schools many years before. Thus, even if charter schools grow rapidly, district-run schools enjoy some buffering from financial pressures. Charter schools in some localities must admit nearly 120 students for the local district to feel the financial consequences of losing 100.

1. Eugenia Toma, Ron Zimmer, and John T. Jones, "Beyond Achievement: Enrollment Consequences of Charter Schools in Michigan," NCSPE Occasional Paper 128, www.ncspe. org (downloaded Jan. 2, 2008).

This buffering cannot last forever. At some point parochial schools will either all close, or they will serve only parents who care enough about the education they offer to be indifferent to the price difference. However, it appears many school districts will benefit from this form of buffering for some time

Nonetheless, some localities are feeling financial pressure. Rustbelt cities with declining populations, and Western cities experiencing gentrification, have many fewer school age children now than in the late twentieth century. These districts would be forced to consider school closures and teacher layoffs even without charter and voucher programs. Districts whose schools have very bad reputations (e.g., Detroit, Milwaukee, and Dayton, Ohio) attract charter school growth, which then further exacerbates existing financial pressures. In a recent study of Milwaukee and Dayton, Christine Campbell and Michael DeArmond show that districts faced with precipitous financial losses ultimately make competitive responses, including investments in school quality, creation of new schools to draw back students, and aggressive elimination of unproductive schools, programs, and people.[2]

Michael Bennet and his successor as Denver superintendent, Tom Boasberg, have recognized that the district is a competitor in a buyer's market for publicly funded schools, and have sought financial efficiencies and instructional improvements to stem the rate of attrition to charters and suburban schools. However, these responses have multiple causes, including histories of enrollment decline that predate the introduction of charter and voucher programs. Charter and voucher programs are attention-getting and give aggressive district leaders a basis to argue that the district must change or die. But without the base of overall district decline, it is unlikely that charters

2. Christine Campbell, Michael DeArmond, Kacey Guin, and Deborah Warnock, *No Longer the Only Game in Town* (Seattle, WA: Center on Reinventing Public Education, University of Washington, 2006).

or vouchers would have caused enough financial pain to any school district to stimulate a competitive response.

Thus, both key supply responses identified in Figure 1—existing schools struggling to improve and new schools emerging—are weakened by the way money flows to schools of choice.

How Much Money Would It Take?

John Merrifield has tried to estimate the amount of money required to stimulate the creation of large numbers of innovative new schools. His results suggest that financial relationships must be at least neutral—that new schools are unlikely to emerge if their established competitors are significantly better funded. He goes further, however, to suggest that there must be positive financial incentives to provide much better schooling than available in public schools.[3]

Given parental inertia and positive sentiments about neighborhood schools, parents are not likely to transfer their children to schools of choice unless they perceive the latter as much better than available district-run schools. Given that many costs of schooling are fixed, it is unlikely that anyone could provide a dramatically better type of school without at least as much money as district-run schools now have available, and possibly more. New schools might emerge to fill particular niches or to serve parents whose children are in particularly egregious public schools, but these will succeed only by not competing with schools serving the majority of children whose parents are not desperately unhappy.

Significant competition from new schools will emerge, Merrifield argues, only when schools that offer something extremely

3. John Merrifield, "Continuous Improvement and Cost Minimization in K–12 Education," draft paper (Seattle, WA: Center on Reinventing Public Education, University of Washington).

attractive can charge more for it. Merrifield suggests that amounts above the local district per-pupil spending could come from tuition or philanthropy. Thus encouraged, innovative school providers would emerge. Existing schools would be forced to compete with them, possibly by finding ways to provide similar services without extra costs. Once in competition, innovative schools would also have to find ways of operating more efficiently.

Merrifield's argument is based on analogy and theory rather than empirical analysis. However, it fits many facts. The most highly touted successes among charter schools, especially the Knowledge Is Power Program (KIPP), extend the scope of services offered and lengthen the school day, both expensive actions paid for with donated services and philanthropic support.

Merrifield does not estimate how much extra would be enough to stimulate new school development, nor does he prove that innovation is impossible at current levels of spending. However, it is clear that charter schools forced to operate with the same or less money than district-run public schools compete as he predicts, by meeting needs not filled by public school programs (e.g., single-sex education), offering safer and more personalized environments, and serving different grade configurations, all low- or no-cost actions. These changes appeal only to a minority of parents, so new schools do not compete with district-run schools across the board.

Other scholars have also asked how much money would be enough to stimulate serious competitive responses from school districts. Dan Goldhaber assessed the incentives implicit in the financial provisions of voucher plans and concluded, "It is uncertain that there has ever been a true test of the market-based competition arguments about vouchers."[4] His analysis would also apply to

4. Dan Goldhaber, "Voucher Finance," in Mark Berends et al., *Handbook of Research on School Choice* (New York: Routledge, 2009), pp. 309-319.

charter schools. As Goldhaber suggests, public schools are likely to be indifferent about financial losses if the cost of a voucher (or the amount transferred to a charter school) is equal to or greater than the marginal cost of educating the students who transfer to schools of choice. However, even a transfer of that size might still be too little to induce school district employees to perceive any threats to their jobs. As Goldhaber argues:

> Annual attrition of teachers from public schools is relatively high, typically in the range of 10–13 percent per year, and it tends to be significantly higher (closer to 20 percent) in high-poverty schools. This high rate of attrition can be used to manage a net loss of students (and the funding that follows them) such that none of the incumbent teachers are actually threatened with job loss.

Goldhaber illustrates the point with an example based on a district that spends an average of $10,000 per pupil:

> A district (or school) losing students is held harmless if those students take $6,000 or less with them upon exit. But given prevailing conditions, schools can probably absorb a significantly larger loss of revenue without harming the personnel who remain. The typical school district, for instance, spends about half its annual operating budget on teacher salaries and benefits (Guthrie & Rothstein, 1999). If the annual teacher attrition rate is 10 percent, then the district budget is automatically reduced by about $500 per pupil; half the $10,000 per pupil cost is spent on teacher salaries and benefits and 10 percent of those teachers leave. This savings could be distributed amongst students receiving a voucher. In other words,

the district could afford to have 20 percent of its students opt to use a voucher worth $8,500 ($6,000 associated with the variable cost of education and $2,500 associated with savings from teacher attrition) without suffering any direct financial consequences. Were teacher attrition to be 20 percent and the voucher take-up rate to be 10 percent, this figure rises to $16,000.

By this reasoning a voucher would have to be much higher than the district's average spending before, holding district enrollment constant, it created a strong incentive for district employees.

Goldhaber's argument meets the test of plausibility. Since the late 1960s, many school districts have lost students steadily, but at a rate slow enough to allow management of the teacher work force by attrition. Dayton's school district serves less than one-third of the students it did in 1965, Seattle's less than 45 percent, and Denver's less than half. Milwaukee, Detroit, and San Francisco have also lost one-third or more of their students. Yet until very recently these districts had not changed their basic financial or program structures, or made any concerted effort to compete with the private, parochial, and suburban public schools to which their students steadily transferred. In the late twentieth century, Seattle experienced such rapid growth of private schools that its proportion of children in private schools went from second from the last in the country to first among major cities. Despite the effects of these changes on district budgets, pressures for competitive responses became strong only when district leaders faced extremely painful choices (e.g., laying off teachers or closing neighborhood schools).

Nothing in this section says exactly how much money must transfer with students to schools of choice in order to fuel the virtuous cycle. Real financial equality with district schools looks like a starting point, not an upper limit. This topic needs a great deal of further work.

It is clear that the basic theory of choice was not nearly specific enough about how much money needs to transfer to schools of choice, and what other factors might help determine whether existing schools strive to improve or good new schools emerge.

CHAPTER 4

QUALITY NEW SCHOOLS ARE RARE, HARD TO START

E mergence of new schools is central to the virtuous cycle, as
Figure 3 shows. New schools motivate and provide an out-
let for innovation, create pressures for existing schools to
improve, and create the demand for new skills that ultimately fuels
the improvement of the teacher force.

From the foregoing discussion of money movement, it is no
surprise that the growth rate of new schools of choice is moderate
at best. The amounts and conditions of funding surely hold down
the numbers of new schools. Equally important are legislative caps
on the numbers of charter schools allowed in particular states and
localities. A slowdown in the numbers of new charter schools during the 2006–2007 school year is evidently caused by caps; the
numbers of charter schools open are approaching the maximum
numbers allowed under current laws. Rapid growth continues
principally in those states (California, New York, Arizona, Florida,

Figure 3

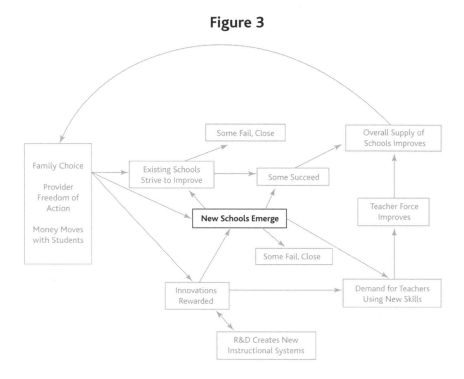

Ohio, and Wisconsin) where caps are far higher than the numbers of charter schools in operation.[1]

Caps are also holding down the numbers of organizations seeking to operate large numbers of charter schools. Organizations such as the nonprofit Charter Management Organizations (CMOs) and the for-profit Education Management Organizations (EMOs) are operating in many states. Yet, their combined capacity is too low to meet an urgent demand for new charter schools, as emerged in New Orleans after Hurricane Katrina. New Orleans was not able to find half as many qualified charter providers as it needed to serve returning students. Consequently, the

1. Jon Christensen and Robin J. Lake in Robin J. Lake, *Hopes, Fears, & Reality in 2007*, Seattle, National Charter School Research Project, p.3.

New Orleans Recovery District has opened more schools the old-fashioned way, as centrally run dependent schools, than as charters. Even places richer in talent and financial capital (e.g., Philadelphia) have struggled to open large numbers of quality charter schools. Though there are many promising new schools in Philadelphia, many operated by apparently qualified providers (e.g., Temple University) have struggled to meet minimum quality standards.

Even without caps and funding limitations, there would still be major lags in time between enactment of policies allowing new schools of choice and actual emergence of schools good enough to attract students and make existing schools feel competitive pressure. The argument that charter schools will be efficient and effective because they have incentives to perform well and freedom to use the most effective methods is a strong one. But even if true in the long run, the argument does not prove out immediately. Entrepreneurs are just learning how to improve charter schools founded only a few years ago, and how to minimize failures, of which there have been many.

Lags are caused in part by student and teacher problems inherited by charter schools and by a weak knowledge base about how to start schools that work well from Day One.

New schools are especially attractive to people who are desperate for alternatives. Many of the teachers, principals, and parents who are quickest to transfer to charter schools were unhappy in their previous schools, are unusual in many ways, and may have hopes and expectations that are difficult to reconcile with school effectiveness. At least some of the staff members who move from public schools to charter schools may be seeking the freedom to teach as they like and to ignore what others do.[2] Socially progressive principals and teachers who staff many charter schools might

2. See Steven F. Wilson, *Learning on the Job: When Business Takes on Public Schools* (Cambridge: Harvard University Press, 2006).

regard individual exploration as a unifying principle more important than instructional coherency. Parents and teachers fleeing violent or chaotic public schools might be willing to settle for safety and order even if instruction is no better than in district-run schools.[3] All parties have to reconcile their diverse expectations and learn to work together—and in some cases, learn they can't work together and either give up or split into more compatible groups.

Unfortunately, though all school districts have opened new schools at one time or another, administrators and scholars have paid little attention to the problems of school start-up. New district-run schools probably also have problems, but little is known about them, so schools of choice are cast as pioneers.

In a small survey of thirty experienced charter school operators conducted by this author, respondents identified three groups of issues that affect all start-up schools:

- New schools must take teachers from many different backgrounds and mold them into a functioning team. This is analogous to the formation of an expansion team in baseball: the new players have different skill levels and some of them might turn out to be very good. But it takes time for the management to figure out how to maximize the overall productivity of the new team and work around its weaknesses (sometimes by making trades).

- Teaching teams mature as they come to agreement about what is to be taught and how, what teachers can expect of

3. Paul Teske suggests that parents seek safety first and feel free to look for more instructionally specific attributes of schools only after safety is assured. See Paul Teske, Jody Fitzpatrick, and Gabriel Kaplan, *Opening Doors: How Low-Income Parents Search for the Right School*, (Seattle,WA: Center on Reinventing Public Education, University of Washington, 2007).

one another, and what work effort and performance should be expected of students.

+ New schools must learn to be very clear in their relationships with parents and students. Charter schools that know what and how they will teach are then able to help parents determine whether the school is the right place for them. Similarly, schools with clear expectations for students can construct students' expectations and increase the school's own leverage on students who try to evade expectations.[4]

In charter schools in particular, hired administrators, lay board members, and founders often struggle for control, leading to leadership turnover and delaying maturation of the instructional program.

These forms of maturation take time but they are not simply a function of years since a school first opened. As sociologist Anthony Bryk has suggested, charter schools that add one grade a year for several years might have 'newness' problems for years after they open. Every year a new group of teachers has to be brought in and informed about the school's values and methods. To a degree, the school must also accommodate itself to the preferences and abilities of the new teachers, at least the ones it needs to keep. These accommodations can happen quickly, or take years. Businesses might have similar issues when opening new facilities or hiring people to expand into new markets.

There is an argument that maturation can't be sped up, and that the numbers of quality new schools can only grow gradually over time. Private school models that have been widely reproduced—the

4. See Paul T. Hill, "The Educational Advantages of Choice," *Phi Delta Kappan*, June 1996.

Yeshivas, Catholic and Quaker schools, branded schools like Montessori—grew organically over a very long time. They developed their own explicit philosophies of instruction, backed up with formal leadership and teacher training, human resource strategies based on hiring alumni whenever possible, and networks to take advantage of expertise widely distributed in schools. These attributes and capacities are not developed quickly or via a few hours of staff training. Individuals invest a great deal in their own training and low-paid apprenticeships. The schools' reputations and moral stances strengthen the hands of management and attract volunteers and donors. The schools seek to influence students' lives twenty-four hours a day, not just during formal instructional hours. Despite all these advantages, some schools overseen by religious and other networks run into trouble and must be taken over and restored or closed.

CMOs and EMOs are trying to reproduce these advantages quickly. These groups try to industrialize school creation, building central capacities to help affiliated schools by reducing the administrative burdens on school leaders, identifying promising teachers and administrators, and training staff in instruction and assessment. Such organizations differ tremendously in what they do for member schools, the amount and quality of what is provided, and how much is spent on central functions. Some do much more to help schools with human resource, administrative, legal, financial, and governance issues than they do to help with instruction. Others emphasize instructional assistance and culture much more. CMOs vary in the forms of help they offer directly, with some allocating large amounts of central staff time to school monitoring and advising and others linking schools with independent sources of help.

The jury is still out on whether CMOs and EMOs are effective in helping schools mature and ultimately increasing school performance.[5] Many CMOs have had great difficulty maintaining quality in large numbers of schools, and have at least temporarily slowed their growth. Based on interviews I have done with CMO heads, it is also clear that concerns for quality and consistency are leading many CMOs to adopt more explicit standards for member schools, encourage less innovation and adaptation to local needs, and create large central office infrastructures that rival school districts in their complexity.

There are some unusually effective EMOs and CMOs, as John Chubb shows. (He identifies KIPP and Edison as especially effective in creating high-performing schools.[6]) But the sources of their effectiveness—inspired leadership, special access to human capital, large investments of capital, capacity for continuous improvement—might prove extremely hard to reproduce at scale. These trends suggest that the industrialization strategy has its limitations as a mechanism to increase the numbers and quality of charter schools. Figuring out how to run a CMO that supports many quality charter schools at scale might be no easier than learning how to run a good charter school.

NewSchools Ventures, a pro-charter organization that has sponsored the creation of many nonprofit CMOs, has just commissioned a study of CMO effectiveness. This study, and self-assessments by for-profit organizations, the most advanced of which is Edison, might start answering the question whether, and if so how, the numbers of new schools started can be increased and their maturation accelerated.

5. James Harvey and Lydia Rainey, *High-Quality Charter Schools at Scale in Big Cities*, Seattle, National Charter School Research Project, 2006. See also Robin J. Lake, *Quantity Counts: The Growth of Charter School Management Organizations*, Seattle, National Charter School Research Project, 2007.

6. John E. Chubb, "Should Charter Schools be a Cottage Industry?" in Paul T. Hill, ed., *Charter Schools Against the Odds* (Stanford: Education Next Books, 2006).

There might be simpler, less expensive, and therefore more sustainable approaches to promoting scale. Organizations with the capacities of CMOs might be available to help schools only on request, and for a fee, obviating the need for complex support organizations and indefinite philanthropic support. Other special purpose organizations might offer targeted forms of help to schools, for example, teacher and administrator registries where schools can find people with experience and positive track records in schools of choice; clearinghouses for parent information about charter school offerings; local colleges that expressly train teachers and principals for charter school work; risk pools that charter schools can join to pool funding for special education services; vendors who can provide insurance and financial services that charter schools need and regular public schools don't; revolving loan funds; real estate trusts that develop properties for rent by schools of choice; information and clearinghouses for quality professional development providers; local transportation companies organized to provide student transportation for schools of choice; and others.

The charter sector is small now and growing slowly. Even if policy barriers like caps on the numbers of schools are lifted, growth is more likely to be steady than explosive. Efforts to accelerate development of new schools, and to industrialize the school-starting process, have encountered their own problems of scaling and quality.

From recent experience, it seems more likely that the choice sector will expand organically than that the numbers of charter and voucher schools can be dramatically expanded by industrial means. However, two events could increase growth in charters and other schools of choice.

First, the No Child Left Behind Act, if reauthorized, could force states and districts to create large numbers of new alternatives for children in low-performing schools. Then the number of people and the amount of financial resources struggling with start-up issues will increase greatly beyond the current investments in charter school start-ups and EMO/CMOs. This could greatly accelerate the virtuous cycle both by increasing change in existing schools and by helping schools of choice. The more people who have experienced school start-up and learned to navigate its snares, the easier it should be for schools of choice to find leaders and sources of assistance. For the moment, however, the choice sector is doing all the heavy lifting. As in other parts of the virtuous cycle, the choice movement can benefit from having school districts take on the same challenges.

This could happen. Alert superintendents and mayors have recognized the inadequacy of any one approach and are implementing a "portfolio strategy," which seeks both to improve existing schools and to create new options. In cities like New York, Chicago, Oakland, California, and Hartford, Connecticut, city leaders have recognized that one size does not fit all. They are "re-missioning" their school districts to operate some schools and work through third parties to provide others, to recruit and train teachers through multiple means, and to experiment with new forms of schooling including uses of technology. The state of Louisiana is building a new system of schools for New Orleans that also uses a combination of chartering, direct operation by a public agency (the Recovery School District), and other methods. Many other cities, including the District of Columbia, Baltimore, Milwaukee, Indianapolis, Denver, Cleveland, and Los Angeles,[7] are also moving toward a deliberate strategy of providing public schools in multiple ways. The conclusion will suggest ways choice supporters can promote complementary changes in school districts.

7. Charles Taylor Kerchner, David Menefee-Libey et al., *Learning from L.A., Institutional Change in American Education* (Cambridge: Harvard University Press, 2008).

The second circumstance under which the numbers of schools of choice could grow more rapidly would be if the focus on innovation were to shift from offering unusually high-touch environments to making greater use of technology. In theory, at least, greater reliance on technology to deliver and manage instruction could increase productivity, simplify replication, accelerate learning about what methods work in what situations, and reduce the need for conventional teaching skills. Being able to teach children more effectively than conventional schools with the same money would give schools of choice a genuinely competitive edge. This would attract families that are now content to leave their children in conventional public schools, therefore driving the virtuous cycle. The next chapter examines that possibility and the conclusion suggests what could make it a reality.

CHAPTER 5

INSTRUCTIONAL
INNOVATION IS SLOW

As with the emergence of new schools, instructional innovation is a central part of the virtuous cycle. As Figure 4 shows, it drives both the emergence of new schools and the improvement of the teaching force.

Opponents of choice claim that charter and voucher schools don't offer anything not already available in public schools, and conclude that there is no justification for moving students and money out of public schools. These claims as stated are easily refuted, as I will show below. However, there is something to the claim that many, perhaps a majority of charters have not offered new forms of instruction, or new ways of using time, technology, or student and teacher work. That is definitely true of private schools that accept vouchers: most are pre-existing schools that do a good job of teaching the old-fashioned way.

Ways Charters Are Innovative

Charters are not just like conventional public schools. Many offer grade configurations (e.g., K–8, 6–12 and K–12) that are difficult

Figure 4

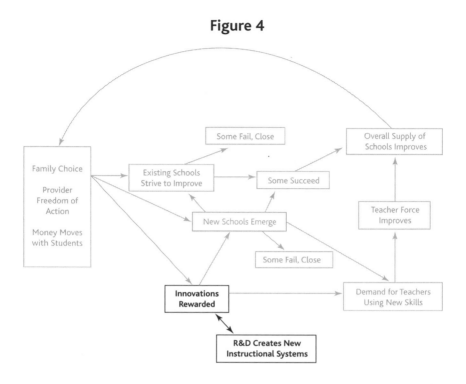

to find in district-run schools, and some bundle social and family services that would otherwise be delivered separately. As Marguerite Roza has shown, some charter schools also take advantage
of the freedom to hire and set salaries to configure their staffs differently. Her comparison of Ohio charter and district-run schools
shows that charters spend higher proportions of their money
on instruction, hire more but younger teachers, hire fewer aides
and full-time specialist teachers, and use contracts for part-time
instructors in music, art, and other specialized subjects.[1] Finally,
as Teske's studies of parental choice behavior have shown, charter

1. Marguerite Roza, Tricia Davis, Kacey Guin, *Spending Choices and School Autonomy: Les-
sons From Ohio Elementary Schools*, Seattle, Center on Reinventing Public Education, School
Finance Redesign Project Working Paper 21, 2007.

schools offer safer and more studious environments, which attract parents whose public school options are bad.

Chester Finn lists many ways in which charter schools can be called innovative, including some mentioned above.[2] Charter schools:

- Offer approaches to instruction that are not available locally (though they might be available in district-run schools elsewhere);
- Mix common instructional practices and student services in unusual ways;
- Give school districts a mechanism for providing schools that union contracts and other constraints would otherwise rule out;
- Allow organizations to form around particular models of schooling (e.g., KIPP) and spread them nationwide;
- Force districts to imitate schools to which many students want to transfer;
- Provide havens for children whose only alternatives are bad or unsafe district-run schools;
- Give districts a mechanism for transforming dysfunctional schools;
- Draw new people into teaching and school leadership;
- Offer "grade configurations that are rare in public school systems, such as schools spanning grades 6–12 and K–12 on a single site, easing or eliminating damaging transitions for kids and giving parents the option of circumventing the middle school entirely."

2. Chester E. Finn, "Chartering and Innovating," in Paul T. Hill, ed., *Charter Schools Against the Odds* (Stanford: Education Next Books, 2006), pp. 159-168.

These illustrations make it clear why parents, especially those whose children are assigned to unsafe or ineffective public schools, seek charters as an alternative, and why state legislators and some school superintendents consider them valuable tools. Superintendents can use chartering as a way to get around the teachers' union contract and provide more rigorous and disciplined schools in the poorest neighborhoods. With a few exceptions, charter schools are most attractive for students whom district schools have failed. District leaders are often happy to see someone else taking on challenges that had beset them and become cause for criticism. Districts often don't fight to keep the students who transfer to charters, and therefore have scant incentives to change their schools in order to compete.

Robin J. Lake identifies an additional way in which charters can be considered innovative—they are intrinsically more open to innovation than district-run schools.[3]

Charter public schools are more likely than district-run public schools to adopt promising practices such as use of technology in the classroom, new staff development programs, involvement of teachers in policy-making, pre-K programs, and parent contracts designed to boost parental involvement.[4] Charters also appear more likely to embrace academic reforms as an integral part of the school mission and not merely as an add-on to the existing program, and they may be more likely to target instructional practices to the most suitable populations. Some argue that this "uptake" function is an essential

3. Robin J. Lake, "In the Eye of the Beholder: Charter Schools and Innovation," *Journal of School Choice*, July 2008.

4. Paul Teske, Mark Schneider, Jack Buckley, and Sara Clark, "Does Charter School Competition Improve Traditional Public Schools?" *Civic Report*, New York, Manhattan Institute, 2000.

aspect of chartering as a policy tool.[5] Charter schools seem to be more likely than other public schools to experiment with unconventional staffing, scheduling, and compensation arrangements and to be responsive to family preferences and needs.

Important though they are, these effects fall short of the original aspirations for schools of choice, which was that innovation would make them more effective than the majority of district-run schools, so that they would attract mainstream students, not just those being served badly. Districts would not want to lose these students and therefore would make schools more attractive and productive in order to keep them.

There is evidence charters could attain this more ambitious goal. In the District of Columbia district-run schools are so turbulent and low-performing, and schools of choice are so numerous, that all groups of students, not just the most disadvantaged, are transferring to charters. The district is losing what it considers its mainstream students, and enrollment is falling rapidly. Under a mayoral take-over, the public school system is fighting to bring back students who have used vouchers and transferred to charters, and union leadership is conflicted over a proposed contract that would establish more flexible and charter-like terms of employment. This, however, is an extreme case given the terrible state of D.C. public schools.

In localities where most public schools are safe, stable, mediocre, but not totally ineffective, the majority of families see no need to transfer. In those cases the schools of choice can drive the virtuous cycle only if they go beyond safety and marginal improvements in instruction to providing more productive schools. Districts need to be forced to compete to hold onto students whose parents are not desperate for options but would be open to something much

5. See Ted Kolderie, "Evaluating Chartering: A Case for Assessing Separately the Institutional Innovation," St. Paul, MN, Education/Evolving, 2003.

better. Charter schools could accomplish this (for example) by seeking more productive tradeoffs between teacher time and technology-based instruction, relying more heavily on online resources, and seeking greater individualization via computer-adaptive testing and targeted tutoring.

There is anecdotal evidence that such things are happening in a few charter schools, but they are too rare to fall into national studies and national databases like the U.S. Department of Education's Schools and Staffing Survey.

To pay their bills, existing charter schools are able to attract enough students who don't fit into conventional public schools or don't feel safe there. They do not need to introduce new approaches to instruction. But if charters are to drive the virtuous cycle, they must draw increasing numbers of students from public schools now considered fair to good.

Why Instructional Innovation Has Lagged

In the early days of the choice movement, formal research and development was not considered necessary because innovation would be a natural consequence of competition. However, as we have seen, nothing is automatic. Charters and voucher-receiving schools have little money or staff capacity to experiment with new approaches to instruction, and little incentive to adopt novel forms of instruction. Even groups of schools organized into for-profit Education Management Organizations (EMOs) and nonprofit Charter Management Organizations (CMOs) have relied on good management of conventional instruction much more than on new forms of instruction or technology.[6]

6. An emerging exception: Edison is reportedly experimenting with uses of online instruction that might reduce the staffing of each of its schools by one or two teachers.

There is little demand for innovation in K–12 education. Unlike other sectors of the economy, in which technology has increased productivity by reducing the numbers of people employed and taking fuller advantage of what only trained professionals can do, public schools now employ more teachers than ever before, and teacher roles have changed little. Past investments in technology have had little effect on the everyday work of public school teachers and administrators. Moreover, state funding schemes, school staffing laws, and teacher certification rules present major barriers to making capital-labor tradeoffs (e.g., between staffing and use of Internet-based instruction). Technology makes changes in teaching and learning possible, but transformation of mainstream education is by no means certain.

There is a growing pool of online curriculum and instructional materials, fueled by online school providers like K–12, state and district-based cyber schools, a big Hewlett Foundation investment in open source resources, and a new Wikipedia-style online sharing community called Curriki (http://www.curriki.org/xwiki/bin/view/Main/WebHome). Though these materials have not been formally assessed, and most cyber schools have at best weak evidence about student learning, there are obviously many possibilities.

And, though cyber schools have grown dramatically, they are still a niche phenomenon, providing options for children who live in remote areas, have dropped out of or refuse to attend conventional schools, or have special needs or responsibilities that make it impossible for them to attend a conventional day school. Despite the growing array of technology-based instructional options, it is not clear whether custodial schools (schools that students attend every day and are under direct adult supervision), including charters, will have incentives to adopt them. The vast majority of parents who send their children to brick-and-mortar schools want constant adult contact, prefer small class sizes to large, and like the idea of a student learning from a teacher. Even if there were powerful technology-based alternatives, they might not be enough to overcome the many sources of resistance in custodial schools.

An argument is just starting to develop between those who think custodial schools won't be able to resist new technology applications as they become available and those who think the technology push alone will not be able to change conventional schools.[7]

The first group includes Clayton Christensen,[8] John Chubb, and Terry Moe,[9] who believe brick-and-mortar schools will not be able to resist increasingly ambitious uses of technology, which will ultimately create new capital-labor tradeoffs that will reduce the numbers of teachers needed and reward new kinds of teaching skills. Moe and Chubb argue that charter and contract schools will adopt productive uses of technology and district-run schools will eventually be forced to follow suit.

Christensen argues by analogy from business competition. Disruptive technologies—products and processes that undermine the demand for an established brand by offering a simpler, cheaper approach that meets the needs of all but the highest-end customers—start by appealing only to customers that the established brand does not serve at all. As the disruptive

---

7. For more detail on the argument presented here, see Paul T. Hill, "Consequences of Instructional Technology for Human Resource Needs in Education," in Dan Goldhaber and Jane Hannaway, eds., *Creating a New Teaching Profession* (Washington, D.C.: Urban Institute Press, 2009), pp. 147-180.

8. Clayton Christensen, Michael B. Horn, and Curtis W. Johnson, *Disrupting Class, How Disruptive Innovation Will Change the Way the World Learns* (New York: McGraw-Hill, 2008).

9. Terry M. Moe and John E. Chubb, *Liberating Learning: Technology, Politics, and the Future of American Education* (San Francisco: Wiley, 2009).

technology improves, it draws more and more customers away from the established brand, thus driving its costs so high that it can no longer compete. Over time the disruptive technology itself becomes the established brand.

To Christensen, cyber schooling fits the image of a disruptive technology. It substitutes technology for expensive labor and it appeals to populations that the conventional public school system neglects—home-schoolers, dropouts, students in remote areas, etc.

This parallel between cyber schools and disruptive business products is impressive, but it misses an important point. In businesses, customers are free to switch from one product to another whenever they like and to re-direct the money they have been spending immediately. This is not the case in K–12 public education. Even when students enroll in cyber schools, some or all of the money available for their instruction stays behind in the conventional schools they left. Cyber schools like Utah's receive their budgets through an entirely different process than regular public schools—they receive a direct state appropriation that is not calibrated as enrollment changes; the conventional schools pay nothing for the cyber school's services. District-run cyber schools cost less than regular district schools, but their students generate the same amount of subsidy from the state as do students in conventional schools. Thus, a district with a cyber school has more, not less, money to devote to its conventional schools. Much the same is true in most states when a cyber charter school competes for district students.

Skeptics (among whom I count myself) think a technology push alone will not transform schools. They do not buy arguments based on tipping points and other transition models based on sectors of the economy that enjoy customer choice and free movement of funds. These conditions do not apply in public education today. Public schools are insulated from the competitive financial pressures that are the active ingredient of Christensen's theory.

Though some districts make competitive responses to charter and voucher-redeeming schools, none has been forced to change its basic operating model. Moreover, districts have proven highly insensitive to loss of enrollment. City school districts like Denver, San Francisco, Oakland, Seattle, Dayton, Cleveland, Salt Lake City and Cincinnati have resisted changing their human resource strategies, labor contracts, and technology uses despite these losses. Moreover, districts that have suffered truly disastrous population losses, like New Orleans and Detroit, are more likely to adopt high-touch models of schooling that maximize adult-student contact, rather than creating efficient classrooms through greater use of technology.

Technology push is important, but not enough by itself to cause fundamental change in methods used in custodial schools. Competition among cyber schools will lead to improvements in their course work and other student services. But that does not mean that custodial schools that serve the majority of students will automatically use what cyber schools develop.

In public school districts, budgetary and interest group politics ensure that for the foreseeable future, technology, no matter how much is purchased, will be used as a supplement to traditional teacher-delivered instruction, not as an alternative to it.

School districts now use computers and link students to online instruction, but only to supplement traditional course work. In the vast majority of custodial schools today, technology does little to change teaching and has few implications for teacher roles, numbers, or skills. These "bolted on" technology uses often happen because legislatures or foundations provide extra funds to purchase computers, software, and Internet connections. But they have little effect on students' core in-school instructional experience or teachers' practice.

The attraction of "bolted on" technologies for conventional public schools is precisely that they do not force change in teacher roles or staffing patterns. Technology uses do not compete for existing funds, and do not affect the numbers of teachers required or the demands made on them. From the perspective of technology vendors, specially funded "bolted on" uses are perfectly acceptable. They create some demand for technology products, enough to create good businesses for some vendors, whether or not the products are used to any effect.

Conventional schools are also protected from technology competition by state legislatures' insistence on segregating expenditures for current services from investments in Research and Development (R&D). Charters and cyber schools are already under attack because they use money for R&D and for salaries of people whom students never see— uses that opponents claim constitute waste or profiteering.[10]

Public policy and funding mechanisms favor stasis, not innovation. State and local funding for K–12 education is now attached to particular programs, buildings, administrative structures, and teachers. Pupils are assigned to particular schools, and even if their parents decide to take them elsewhere, the sending school and the teachers it employs are protected from financial losses. Even if school leaders would like to innovate they are not free to cash in teacher salaries or other mandated expenditures in favor of new

10. See Luis A. Huerta, Chad D'Entremont, and Maria Fernanda Gonzales, "Perspectives on Cyber and Homeschool Charters," in Mark Berends, et al., *Handbook of Research on School Choice* (New York: Routledge, 2009), pp. 533-554

kinds of purchases. Thus, public funding is not neutral about supporting technical innovations, but biased against them.

Teachers in conventional schools can use technology to supplement and enrich instruction, without changing their basic instructional methods or creating cost advantages for their schools. Cyber schools might serve a growing niche audience but they cannot meet the needs of the majority of families that need their children cared for during the working day, or of students who need close supervision.

Moe and Chubb are extremely clear about teacher unions' blocking ability.[11] They might also have pointed out that the whole public education system is structured to prevent schools from using money to purchase goods and services other than those on a narrowly prescribed list. Thus defended in depth, the current system is highly resistant to change. Moe and Chubb lay out a plausible scenario under which technology weakens union power, which then leads to erosion of the system's other defenses. It is, however, hard to believe that such a transition could be quick. Even if some localities make dramatic shifts from the existing system to one that exploits technology to make schools more productive, other localities could take decades to make the change.

Pathways to Innovation

Full exploitation of technology in custodial schools will require changes in politics, in funding, and in the ways technology is applied. Moe and Chubb provide a masterful analysis of the political preconditions. I discuss needed changes in financing in Chapter 7.

11. See *Liberating Learning*, chapters 3 and 5.

Technology must not be used as a small supplement to current methods of instruction. Rather, it should become the basis of something new: integrated instructional systems that redesign teacher and student work, such that most formal instruction is provided online and individually paced. The teacher's work will consist of diagnosis, enrichment, and leadership of group interactions. Students would encounter information via technical means, but teachers would track students' work and intervene when needed.

Teachers would need to interpret student performance assessments, know what technology-based supplementary resources were available and what they were good for, and decide when to use supplementary resources and when to provide personal tutoring or coaching.

Integrated instructional systems would take full advantage of both technology-based delivery and in-person teacher-student and student-student interaction. The teacher would use technical means whenever possible, reserving his own time and attention for intervention for things only he could do such as explain an idea in a way not provided by the text or digital materials, intervene with an individual student, frame group work, or call attention to productive differences in ways different students approach a task.

Despite the dramatic growth in possible instructional technologies, it is still necessary to ask whether and at what rate technological developments are likely to penetrate custodial public and private schools. Will technology-based instruction remain a niche phenomenon limited to cyber schools serving marginal populations, with only marginal uses in mainstream schools? Or can competition force innovative technology-based forms of instruction into mainstream schools?

None of these sources of pressure is particularly strong today, and all face significant challenges. Though in the very long run technology is likely to infiltrate all forms of education, we might be many years from the sort of technology revolution heralded by Christensen and others.

The most important thing government can do to encourage technology innovation in schools is to pay for results, for example, courses completed or student credits generated, rather than for the costs of service delivery. Technology-based instruction should be cheaper to deliver than more conventional teacher-intensive instruction, but it requires significant expenditures in research, development, and testing. Government must pay for instruction in ways that support investment. To be as effective as it can be, technology-based instruction must be subject to continuous improvement, including occasional abandonment of methods and equipment that were once state of the art. Entities that develop truly superior modes of instruction must also be able to make profits and use them as the basis for raising investment capital or selling stock.

If government paid for education in the ways described, an active marketplace for technology-based instruction would surely emerge, generating significant spending on research and development. More flexible government funding for education could also generate private human resource investments needed to create a supply of teachers and school leaders with the requisite skills, and therefore to help drive the virtuous cycle.

As I argue below,[12] in the absence of dramatic changes in the ways government pays for education, technology development will

12. See also Paul T. Hill, "Spending Money When It Is Not Clear What Works," *Peabody Journal of Education*, 83, no. 2, 2008. See also Anthony S. Bryk, "Ruminations on Reinventing an R&D Capacity for Educational Improvement," prepared for the American Enterprise Institute Conference, "The Supply Side of School Reform and the Future of Educational Entrepreneurship," October 25, 2007.

also require major government or philanthropic investments in R&D to subsidize development and proof of highly effective new technology-based instructional systems. Under current government funding policies, school districts and groups of independent schools lack the funds to support the needed search for technology options and development and testing of prototype systems.

CHAPTER 6

INFLUENCE ON THE EDUCATIONAL LABOR FORCE IS SLIGHT

The virtuous cycle model predicts that choice will lead to general improvement of the teaching force, first by attracting a new supply of teachers with skills and attitudes that lead to more effective instruction, and second by making district-run public schools seek similar teachers in order to compete. Though district-run schools are constrained by union contracts and state teacher certification requirements, public education leaders will be forced to find ways around these limitations—by using chartering to hire teachers in new ways or by forcing changes in laws and contracts.

As this chapter will show, all these predictions have come true, to a degree. Charter schools have tapped into promising new sources of teachers, and a few school districts are using chartering to work around their collective bargaining agreements. In the District of Columbia, competition neutralized local but not national union opposition to a proposed collective bargaining agreement that would make teachers' jobs contingent on performance.

However, these events are extremely rare and limited to the boundaries of the few most embattled school districts. Moreover, it is still far from clear that even these few districts can attract enough new teachers, or cause enough incumbent teachers to change their attitudes and re-tool their skills, to make a significant change in the quality of the teacher labor force.

New Sources of Teachers

Charter and voucher-funded schools have greater freedom than district-run schools to decide how many teachers they want, choose the individuals they want to hire, and make work assignments consistent with the school's instructional program and students' needs. These schools can also more readily counsel unproductive people out of teaching and fill vacancies with the best people they can get. Given that schools of choice depend on their reputations to attract students, it makes sense that they would hire the best people available rather than, as most district-run schools must do, hire whomever the district's teacher placement rules designate for them.

Freedom over teacher hiring is a competitive advantage for schools of choice. Charter and voucher schools should be able to attract students based on reputations for effective teaching and motivated staffs. They should also be able to use their freedom to set pay and create positive working conditions to get and keep unusually good teachers. Schools of choice should also seek competitive advantages by developing new, more productive roles for teachers[1] (e.g., via uses of technology).

To a degree, choice has opened up teaching to more able individuals who have greater career ambitions and are more likely to

1. Michael Podgursky and Dale Ballou, *Personnel Policy in Charter Schools*, Washington D.C., Thomas B. Fordham Foundation, 2001.

seek the economic advantages that come from high performance. Public school teachers are now an isolated group as distinctive as the military, with their own ideology and with life experiences as members of an economically insulated bureaucracy. Other college-educated citizens are much more likely to change careers several times and to experience competitive economic pressures and rewards for self-improvement and high performance.[2] Increasing the numbers of people from outside the traditional teaching roles could, at least in theory, lead to teachers who innovate and invest in their own skills, and to schools that respond positively to performance pressures.

Charter and voucher schools do draw teachers with distinctive skills and backgrounds. For example, charter schools are more likely to employ graduates of competitive colleges and individuals who have college training in mathematics and science.[3] Charter teachers are also younger on average, have much less teaching experience (more than 60 percent have five or fewer years of teaching experience compared to 26 percent of public school teachers), and are more likely to be members of minority groups.[4] Charter teachers have completed more science and mathematics coursework than teachers in conventional public schools[5] and are less likely to have graduated from a traditional school of education. They are also less likely than conventional public school teachers (by 72 percent to

2. See Sarah Brooks, "Taking Advantage of Teacher Turnover," in Paul T. Hill and James Harvey, eds., *Making School Reform Work: New Partnerships for Real Change* (Washington, D.C.: Brookings Institution Press, 2003).

3. Caroline M. Hoxby, "Would School Choice Change the Teaching Profession?" *Journal of Human Resources,* 37 (4, fall), 2002, pp. 846-891.

4. Dominic Brewer and Jane Ahn, "What Do We Know about Teachers in Charter Schools?" in Julian R. Betts and Paul T. Hill, eds., *Taking Measure of Charter Schools,* Seattle, National Charter School Research Project, Center on Reinventing Public Education, 2010.

5. Caroline M. Hoxby, "Would School Choice Change the Teaching Profession?" *Journal of Human Resources,* 37(4), 2002, pp. 846-891.

93 percent) to have teaching certificates.[6] Moreover, as Dominic Brewer has noted:

> Early case study reports of Arizona charter schools found that charters hired teachers with outside experience in relevant subject matter areas. For example musicians, artists, or engineers were hired to teach music, art, and science classes.

Table 1 summarizes the results of a new comparison between charter and non-charter public school teachers in Ohio, based on work led by Betheny Gross.

Effects on the Teaching Labor Force

Another hope is that the teaching force will become increasingly populated by individuals who understand what it means to work in an organization where all professionals stand or fall together based on combined performance, and where jobs depend on customer choices—an organization that is required to create and live up to a definite image and reputation. Teachers with these attitudes could profoundly affect district-run schools in which teachers habitually work as isolated individuals. Teachers' union leaders fear this will happen.[7] The NEA abandoned its own foray into charter management in San Diego when it concluded that unionized teachers who had tasted the freedom of working in a charter school were

6. M. Burian-Fitzgerald, M.T. Luekens, and G.A. Strizek, "Less Red Tape or More Green Teachers: Charter School Autonomy and Teacher Qualifications," in K. E. Bulkley and P. Wohlstetter, eds., *Taking Account of Charter Schools: What's Happened and What's Next?* (New York: Teachers College Press, 2003).

7. For an examination of clashing views about appropriate teacher roles, see Paul T. Hill, Lydia Rainey, and Andrew J. Rotherham, "The Future of Charter Schools and Teachers Unions," National Charter School Research Project, 2006.

Table 1: Ohio Charter Teachers are Younger, Less Likely to have Advanced Degrees, and Less Likely to be Certified

	CHARTER SCHOOL AVERAGE	NON-CHARTER PUBLIC SCHOOL AVERAGE
Age	34	41
% Female	74%	73%
With Masters	21%	55%
Fully Certified	79%	97%

reluctant to return to bureaucratic jobs. Former United Federation of Teachers President Randi Weingarten has taken serious criticism from other union leaders for her "risky" decision to accept management responsibility for some charters in New York state.

However, as with other predictions drawn from the virtuous cycle model, expectations that schools of choice would kick off a transformation of the overall teaching force have not worked out as expected. This is so in part because of problems already discussed, especially limitations in the number and quality of new schools and relatively little instructional innovation. But there are additional, unexpected problems.

Charter schools are having serious trouble finding and keeping sufficient numbers of qualified people. In cities with many charters, school heads find themselves competing desperately with one another for the same young people who want to do a few years' service in the classroom. Thousands of college graduates who might have gone into other careers teach in charter schools for a while. But as the numbers of charter schools increase, the need for such teachers threatens to outstrip the supply.

Charter schools also draw nearly half their teachers from district-run schools. Though there is no formal study of how such teachers work out in charter schools, there is ample anecdotal evidence that many former district school teachers have serious problems adjusting. Many conventional teachers come with expectations about responsibility for process not results, and expectations for unconditional job security that are incompatible with the needs of a school working in a harsh competitive environment. Though some adapt, many last only a short time before realizing that the burdens of charter teaching are not for them.

State charter laws in twenty-one states also discourage district-employed teachers from giving charter schools a try, by limiting the seniority credit and pension amounts they can accrue while working in charters.[8]

Alumni of Teach For America (TFA) and The New Teacher Project (TNTP) are important recruits for charter schools, but their numbers are small compared to the need. The importance of TFA alumni to schools run by CMOs is illustrated by the fact that eighty of 250 CMO-affiliated schools have TFA alumni in leadership positions and eighty-seven (31 percent) employ TFA alumni as teachers. However, charter schools not affiliated with CMOs have much less access to TFA alumni. Fewer than 5 percent (167) of nearly 3,500 non-CMO affiliated charter schools have TFA alumnus teachers.[9] Moreover, even if every TFA alumnus (instead of about one in ten at present) went to work in a charter school, they could provide only about 2,500 of the more than 10,000 new teachers whom existing charters must hire each year.

8. Dominic Brewer and Jane Ahn, "What Do We Know about Teachers in Charter Schools?" in Julian R. Betts and Paul T. Hill, eds., *Taking Measure of Charter Schools*, Seattle, National Charter School Research Project, Center on Reinventing Public Education, 2010.

9. TFA figures are based on the author's analysis of alumni placement summaries provided by Teach For America.

High rates of teacher turnover exacerbate the gap between the numbers needed and available.[10] Estimates of teacher turnover in charter schools range from as much as 42 percent per year to as little as 25 percent. As Gary Miron reports, younger teachers, individuals with little prior teaching experience, and non-certified teachers are more likely to leave a charter school at the end of any given year than older, more experienced, and certified teachers. Older teachers and those with education beyond a bachelor's degree were more likely to stay in their charter schools.

Miron's analysis does not compare teacher turnover in charter schools with district-run schools serving similar students. Other analyses suggest that district-run schools situated in low-income neighborhoods and serving heavily minority populations have similar rates of turnover.[11] However, the fact remains that charter schools must recruit a large number of teachers every year just to maintain their teaching forces. (A recent study shows that charter schools are also challenged to replace founders and other school heads, who depart at a rate approaching 20 percent, and that existing training programs for charter leaders produce only a small fraction of the numbers needed.)[12]

These results are not surprising in light of charter schools' appeal to young people just out of college and to Teach For America and AmeriCorps alumni, many of whom are planning to enter graduate school and pursue other careers. Based on a new Ohio

10. See Gary Miron and Brooks Applegate, "Teacher Attrition in Charter Schools," Education Policy Research Unit, Arizona State University, 2008. Compare Dale Ballou and Michael Podgursky, "Teacher Recruitment and Retention in Public and Private Schools," *Journal of Policy Analysis and Management*, 17(3), June, 1998, pp. 393-417.

11. Kacey Guin, "Chronic Teacher Turnover in Urban Elementary Schools," *Education Policy Analysis Archive*, 12, no. 24, 2004.

12. Christine Campbell and Brock J. Grubb, *Closing the Skill Gap: New Options for Charter School Leadership Development*, Seattle, National Charter School Research Project, 2008.

survey, Betheny Gross and colleagues at the Center on Reinventing Public Education report that 77 percent of teachers who leave charter schools go into work other than teaching. Some might return to teaching later in their careers, but for the moment they leave holes that are extremely difficult to fill. Charter schools scramble to fill their own vacancies and add few teachers to the labor force serving district-run public schools.

Based on early results from Gross' ongoing study of charter school operations, mature schools might be developing human resource strategies that can cope with turnover. These involve keeping some teachers for long periods of time, so they can socialize new teachers about the school's identity and approach to instruction, but also anticipating that the majority of new young teachers hired will leave after an average of two years. Many private schools use similar strategies as a necessary way to control salary costs. Miron's evidence is consistent with this analysis. Attrition rates among teachers who have been in a given charter school for three years or more are below 20 percent, and attrition among teachers over fifty years of age is below 25 percent. Attrition is also much lower in charter schools that have operated for three years or more than in new schools.

The mixed senior/junior strategy is possible only if schools are able to identify and hold onto the teachers best suited to internal leadership roles. Charter schools that offer extremely low pay and treat teachers as commodities—and there are some—have little chance to solve the turnover problem.

Though there is some movement from charters to conventional district schools, the numbers are small. Undoubtedly, some teachers who transfer to district-run schools take along the non-bureaucratic values experienced in charter schools. However, as Miron shows, teachers who leave charters are more than three times as likely to be dissatisfied with the school's mission statement and with the way the charter school is governed than teachers who stay. Former public school teachers who try working in charters are also much more likely to leave charters than are teachers from other backgrounds. Thus, charter school teachers who leave for public school jobs are more likely to adapt to public school norms than to be missionaries for the kinds of working environments and performance incentives implicit in charter-style teacher employment.

Nor is there any evidence that school districts see charters as a place to recruit teachers. Districts do not see any need to seek teachers with the skills and attitudes developed in charter schools, and are not training their own teachers in ways charters need.

The foregoing raises the question whether choice can have any fundamental effect on the public school district teaching force. Given high rates of turnover, existing charters might always struggle to fill their teaching slots, and continually lose teachers to jobs outside education. Charter expansion in any locality might be strictly limited by the numbers of college graduates willing to spend a few years teaching, and by the numbers of public school teachers willing to temporarily try something new.

Localities like the District of Columbia and New Orleans have been able to attract volunteers from across the country, but it is not clear whether they have increased the national pool of such people, or only forced its reallocation.

Teacher Supply and the Virtuous Cycle

The depiction of causal relationships in Figure 1 (p. 4) might be much too simple: the human resource pool might improve only after competition forces districts to increase school-level autonomy and performance accountability, and therefore to invest in recruiting and training large numbers of individuals who can work effectively under those conditions.

With the exception of the few large districts that have adopted choice and new schools as reform mechanisms (e.g., Chicago, New York, District of Columbia, Hartford, Connecticut, and New Orleans), school districts have not rushed to hire teachers from sources other than education schools. When districts look for new supplies of teachers, they turn to state-authorized alternative certification programs that provide essentially the same training—and are as objectionable to high-ability young college graduates—as traditional education school programs. Rather than seek to increase the numbers of teachers like those in charter schools, school district leaders, deans of conventional education schools, and teachers' union heads are content with the old ways and comforted by the difficulties charter schools encounter. They are not likely to abandon the old model of career teachers with civil service status any time soon. Except in the few cities where charter competition has put districts under serious financial pressure, districts and teachers' unions have found it easy to resist giving school-level leaders the charter-like freedom to hire and assign teachers.

Some significant changes in the teaching force are coming from new training programs designed to provide teachers for beleaguered inner-city districts. Teach For America and The New Teacher Project are supplying many teachers that schools of choice might eventually be able to attract. But these programs arise from the broader performance pressures on districts, mostly due to the No Child Left Behind Act and state accountability programs, not from pressures caused by choice.

Choice might still affect the overall quality of the teaching force. Older charter schools have lower rates of teacher turnover, suggesting that as charter schools mature the annual scramble for new teachers to fill vacancies will ease. Further, the longer individuals work as charter school teachers, the more likely they are to continue teaching, whether in the charter school for which they were first hired or in some other school. Young people who worked in charter schools for a few years after graduating from college might also try teaching again later in their careers, swelling the ranks of charter-style teachers. Thus, the predicted effects on the teaching force might still occur, though with significant lags.

Chapter 7 suggests ways policymakers and pro-choice philanthropists can improve charter schools' access to teachers and enhance the effects of choice on the overall teacher supply.

CHAPTER 7

BAD SCHOOLS DON'T ALWAYS CLOSE

Choice is a destructive process as well as a creative one. In all but the fastest growing localities, new schools can emerge and prosper only if they are able to draw students away from other schools. The numbers of students and amounts of money that can move to new and better schools are limited. Opportunities for new schools and their effects on overall student performance will be strictly limited if the worst schools stay open and continue using resources and teaching students.

Figure 5 illustrates the place of school closures in the virtuous cycle. Effects on overall school quality, emergence of new schools, innovation, and improvement of the teacher labor market all depend in part on closure of unsuccessful schools to free up dollars, students, and teachers for new ones.

In a fully developed market, customers learn quickly about better options, control their own purchasing decisions, and can therefore switch easily. Nothing can sustain a product or company that

Figure 5

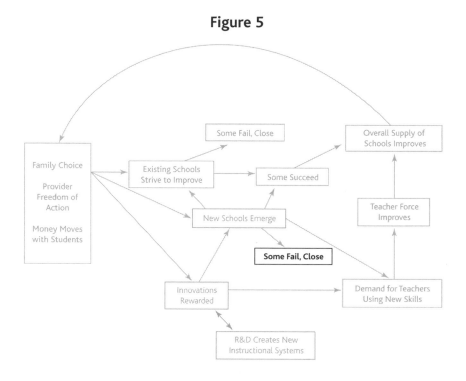

has lost its customer base. K–12 education was not built on market principles. Today information is limited, customers base decisions on complex criteria, and switching is difficult. Public school districts make it difficult to transfer between schools, and families that choose schools outside their neighborhoods must often assume transportation burdens.[1]

Local politics also inhibits some choices, as neighborhood leaders press parents to keep their children in particular schools to avoid the loss of a perceived community asset. Teachers' unions and community groups oppose closure of low-performing district-run schools, citing jobs, tradition, and resistance to externally imposed

1. See Paul Teske, Jody Fitzpatrick, and Tracey O'Brien, *Drivers of Choice: Parents, Transportation, and School Choice* (Seattle, WA: Center on Reinventing Public Education, University of Washington, 2009).

standards. Low-performing charter schools also get political support from vendors, teachers, and neighborhood leaders.

Despite the No Child Left Behind Act's requirements that the worst schools be closed and replaced, few districts are doing anything of the sort. In 2004-2005, only seventy-five district-run schools nationwide were in the restructuring phase required by NCLB, and none had been closed. Schools are closed, but usually because of declining enrollments or facilities decay. Aside from Oakland, New York, and Chicago, which have each closed tens of schools as part of their own new schools' initiatives (and New Orleans where schools were closed by forces of nature), the numbers of schools that have been closed for reasons of poor performance have been in the tens.

Districts' ability to sustain their worst schools is a major drag on the virtuous cycle. Closing a school forces reassignment of tenured teachers, displaces an administrative staff, and can upset school board members from the affected parts of the city. It is therefore much easier for district leaders to sustain a bad school, rationalizing that additional professional development for teachers or some new program will turn it around.

The persistence of weak schools of choice also limits opportunities for new schools. Though charter schools are much likelier to close than district-run schools, still only 107 of nearly 3,800 charters closed in 2006-2007.[2] The states of California, Arizona, and Florida accounted for 60 percent of all charter school closures. The vast majority of these closures were due to financial or personnel mismanagement, problems correlated with (but not identical to) low instructional effectiveness. Data on voucher-redeeming schools are harder to find. Very weak private schools have closed

2. Jon Christensen in Robin J. Lake, ed., *Hopes, Fears, & Reality: A Balanced Look at American Charter Schools in 2007*, Seattle, National Charter School Research Project, 2007, p.4.

in Milwaukee, Dayton, and Cleveland, and some of their students have transferred to better funded and presumably more stable char-ter schools. However, these transactions have effectively reduced charter schools' competitive effects on district-run schools.

Due to state caps, the numbers of charter schools that can be opened in any locality are limited. If many charter schools are weak or unattractive, charter schools can exert even less competitive pressure on district-run schools than their numbers would suggest. There is evidence that a significant proportion of charter schools are in fact low-performing. Two recent studies, by Julian Betts and Margaret Raymond, suggest that charter schools are more variable in quality than district-run public schools.[3] Betts:

> Broadly speaking, there is ample evidence that charter schools in some areas outperform traditional public schools, and, to a slightly lesser degree, that charter schools under-perform in other areas. There are far more significantly positive and sig-nificantly negative charter school effects in the value-added and lottery literature than we would expect if charter schools were never different from traditional public schools.
>
> The mission of charter schools is to offer innovative curri-cula and teaching methods. The finding of considerable het-erogeneity among charter schools probably reflects this spirit of innovation and experimentation. Of course, this begs the question of whether over time the weaker charter schools will shrink or close, while the better charter schools expand . . .

3. Julian R. Betts and Y. Emily Tang, "Value-Added and Experimental Studies of the Ef-fect of Charter Schools on Student Achievement: A Literature Review," in Robin J. Lake, *Hopes, Fears, & Reality: A Balanced Look at American Charter Schools in 2008*, Seattle, Na-tional Charter School Research Project, 2008. Margaret Raymond, *Multiple Choice: Charter School Performance in Sixteen States*, Stanford, Center for Research on Educational Outcomes (CREDO), 2009.

Second, in a few cases the evidence to date is quite one-sided. For instance, elementary charter schools seem to be producing better gains in reading achievement than traditional public schools. Similarly charter middle schools often outperform in math. Conversely, charter high schools seem to lag behind traditional public schools, especially in math. We urgently need more rigorous studies at the high school level.

Third, the overall evidence suggests that charter schools more typically outperform than under-perform their traditional public school counterparts.

As both Raymond and Betts suggest, these findings highlight the importance of closing the lowest-performing charter schools. They are as big a drag on the virtuous cycle as are low-performing district-run schools that no one does anything about.

Betts' and Raymond's results make sense of two previously conflicting perceptions: first, that many charter schools offer quality options not otherwise available; and, second, that charter performance on average is not particularly high.

Why Weak Schools Aren't Closed

For both district-run schools and schools of choice, there are three barriers to closure of bad schools: muted parental response, provider resistance, and non-functioning oversight bodies.

Muted parental response: Parents are often reluctant to transfer students, whether from regular public, charter or private schools, except when students are in danger of harm or are unhappy. When parents do switch schools they often look for attributes other than average school performance. These can be safety, studiousness of climate, individualization, professed ability to help students who fall behind, or openness to children with a given ethnic identity or educational need.

Even privileged tuition-paying parents try to match a school with a child's interests and perceived needs. Studying the process of choice among parents who apply to charter schools, Paul Teske concluded that their goals and criteria were very like those of parents paying private school tuition. However, the schools to which their children were assigned were much worse, and the options they considered—limited by transportation and a desire to avoid placement in a school where their child would be the sole member of his or her minority group—were much more limited.[4] The result is that few parents start at the top of the test score list and work downward. Parents with more than one child often seek different schools for each, depending on individual children's traits.

Tuition-paying parents normally choose among schools that are able to educate their students reasonably effectively. However, parents choosing charter and voucher schools, often concerned with escaping unsafe or instructionally chaotic schools, often settle for something only a little better. This helps explain parents' loyalty to district and charter schools that are low-performing by standard measures, but offer safe and caring environments. Believing their children cannot learn in chaotic places, they grab what they can and hold onto it. This helps explain the persistence of significant numbers of low-performing charter schools.

As Teske has suggested, there may be ways to open up low-income and disadvantaged parents' choice-sets by exposing potential choosers to parents like themselves who have sent children to schools outside their normal zone of consideration, and by arming

4. Paul Teske and Robert Reichardt, "Doing Their Homework: How Charter School Parents Make Their Choices," in Robin J. Lake, ed., *Hopes, Fears, & Reality: A Balanced Look at American Charter Schools in 2006*, Seattle, National Charter School Research Project, 2006.

community opinion leaders with rich data about how poor and minority children fare at a large number of schools.[5]

Provider resistance: This does not need a subtle explanation. Individuals leading and teaching in low-performing schools are reluctant to lose jobs or be forced to find new posts. Many also believe in the mission and core ideas around which their school was founded, and are reluctant to give up on them. Staff members in conventional public schools can also be outraged when what they thought was an unconditional job assignment is threatened.

Charter school founders, many of whom made financial sacrifices to start a school, also have incentives to "dig in" in response to evidence of low performance. Schools run by larger organizations— youth-oriented nonprofits trying their hand at formal education, community-based organizations, and EMOs/CMOs—also have strong incentives to avoid financial losses and resist being tagged as failures. The best EMOs and CMOs are willing to abandon failures, but others can also strongly resist closure of bad schools.

The dig-in response is particularly strong among school founders who professedly do not believe in tests and have built their schools on the premise that what counts can't be measured. Though there are high-performing progressive and community-based charter schools, a significant number of troubled charters are run and staffed by people who place themselves in opposition to what they perceive as the dominant culture.

The same beliefs can buttress teachers' union opposition to school closures.

Unlike parents, whose resistance to school closure can be muted if they can see better options, providers have the most to

5. Paul Teske, Jody Fitzpatrick, and Gabriel Kaplan, *Opening Doors: How Low-Income Parents Search for the Right School* (Seattle, WA: Center on Reinventing Public Education, University of Washington, 2006).

lose and are likely to resist school closures as strongly as they can. Their resistance can only be overcome by strong public oversight. Unfortunately, school districts and charter authorizers are often not equipped to judge school performance or willing to endure opposition to closure decisions.

Non-functioning oversight bodies: In an earlier Hoover Press book, Chester Finn and this author observed:

> Authorizers, aka sponsors, were the most neglected part of the charter school phenomenon in the early days. Though it would be an exaggeration to say that these new schools were expected to come into existence via immaculate conception, their parentage received scant attention . . . Even such primal charter-school theorists as the late Ray Budde and Albert Shanker paid little attention to the subject of sponsorship. They focused more on innovative schools than novel governance arrangements.

More recently, the National Association of Charter School Authorizers (NACSA) has worked to raise standards for charter authorizing, showing how oversight bodies could rigorously assess proposals for new schools and monitor the performance of new schools. Though some NACSA members still act as though an authorizer's job is to support charter schools through thick and thin, others are adopting higher oversight standards and learning how to close schools.

Though charter authorizers are just starting to learn how to judge schools and manage the backlash from closures, they are far ahead of school districts.

NCLB and state standards-based reform polities make it urgent that school districts develop the capacity for performance-based oversight. Moreover, the need to stem student population losses is increasing pressure on districts to oversee schools on the basis of performance. District leaders are forced to ask, "What about our schools is causing people to leave? Are all of our schools a problem or just some? What can we do to improve the district's schools and its reputation?"

The answer to these questions inevitably involves judging schools and then acting to improve existing schools, create attractive new options, or both.

Performance-based oversight redefines accountability in public education. Traditionally, school districts have equated accountability with measurement: they tested students and made schools' results public. This put pressure on educators and caused parents to complain or seek transfers. Many districts tried to upgrade low-performing schools via leadership changes and staff development, but if those remedies did not work, the same schools continued to operate. Performance-based accountability puts the burden on districts, as on charter authorizers, to make judgments and to find or develop better options until every student is in an effective school.

Performance-based oversight requires school districts and charter authorizers to meet a number of high standards.

They must not just provide schools, but provide schools that will *educate children effectively*. They must not just make a reasonable effort and then give up, but *work relentlessly for performance*. It's not enough to provide a school that has good parts and therefore should work; districts and authorizers need to make sure *every school works*.

Schools today must go beyond providing what children needed to know a generation ago when school board members and many teachers were educated; they must keep track of changes in higher education and the economy and adjust the set of schools offered in a community so children learn what they will need. With respect to disadvantaged children and newcomers (immigrants, refugees), educators should go beyond providing schooling that would be sufficient for middle-class and native-born Americans. Their task extends to *searching and experimenting* until children get what they need to succeed.

Accountability means more than providing performance incentives for educators. Rewards and punishments are only tools (and not always the most important ones) that districts can use to improve children's educational opportunities. Other methods (e.g., experimentation with new forms of schooling, using new mixes of technology and teacher work) are also tools that districts need to be able to use. Finally, districts and authorizers must be able to run their own schools and sponsor and oversee schools run by others. Moreover, they need to oversee all schools, no matter who runs them, via common performance standards and methods of oversight.

This goes far beyond what Americans have traditionally expected of school districts.

Moreover, districts need to repeat the cycle indefinitely. Students' needs and characteristics change, so that a set of schools that was perfectly adequate for one period may be inadequate later. Existing schools sometimes decline after long periods of acceptable performance, but new schools are not sure to work. Thus, assessing the mix of schools a district offers needs to be a way of life, not a one-time event.

With respect to school closures, it is clear that there is no replacement for competent government oversight of schools. This is a radical departure from the way most districts operate today. Most assume that they operate a stable set of schools that changes only when population shifts require opening new schools in neighborhoods with

growing student populations or closing schools with very low enrollment. Few districts make concerted efforts to develop alternative
schools or replace low-performing ones.

Chicago, New York, and Philadelphia are partial exceptions:
they have used chartering and contracting out to develop some
new options and replace some schools. No district has applied the
performance oversight process sketched here to all its schools.

The virtuous cycle requires school closures, but for the foreseeable future these will result as much or more from governmental
action than through pure market processes. This introduces a main
theme of the final chapter: for choice to achieve its full potential
effects on America's public schools, states and school districts must
be enlisted to perform key functions.

CHAPTER 8

CHOICE CAN MOVE
MORE RAPIDLY

M any things block or delay the virtuous cycle. Some of them are intrinsic to the choice process itself: it takes time for educators to break old habits and to learn how to take advantage of the freedoms provided by choice, and for families to learn how to make smart choices of schools. Other blockages are caused by policies and regulations, many deliberately imposed by opponents, but some accepted by choice supporters without full understanding of their consequences. Opponents imposed caps on the numbers of charter schools, but choice supporters agreed to accept low per-pupil funding in charter and voucher programs, mistakenly assuming that independent school providers could do more for less than district-run schools.

Choice can lead to the virtuous cycle described in Chapter 1, but the conditions need to be right. People must be able to exercise choices and money must move when they do. Even then progress can be slow, just as in other fields. There was no place for Southwest Airlines as long as the federal government controlled airfares and regulated the industry on behalf of the big carriers.   After deregulation it took a long time for someone to come up with a new service model that could survive and prosper. Moreover, even with Southwest as a model, new lower-cost carriers (including those started by United and Delta) have trouble surviving economic downturns and rises in fuel prices. The legacy carriers, troubled though they are, still have huge assets and dominate air service to many markets, despite their high costs, inefficiency, and lack of imagination. Southwest makes it clear that the virtuous cycle can work in the airline business. But after many years the cycle is just getting started, and only a few people are better off.

The market's invisible hand is a nice image, but introducing the virtuous cycle to an industry dominated by government or government-protected enterprise requires visible action of many kinds. Real people must raise capital, abandon other work, hire talented people into chancy jobs, and develop service designs and business models. Doing these things is very difficult. Take the first, raising capital: Edison Schools did well in the equities market until investors became convinced that the policy environment was too hostile to allow the company to make big returns. Then the stock fell and the company had to go private. The other tasks are risky enough that under some circumstances few or no people will undertake them.

Some individuals who take on the risks of starting new schools might know what they are getting into but others might not. Thus failures are likely. Even when the conditions are marginally favorable (e.g., in the airline industry) it can take a long time for even one good new entrant to arise and affect existing providers.

In the meantime, people who think market-like phenomena are necessary preconditions for progress in K–12 education can do more than theorize and wait. It is not too late for opponents to push the choice movement back into marginality, by attacking charter laws and piling more money onto bureaucratically run school districts. Those who think choice must happen must be willing to press for policies that create a competitive environment, and to strategize, invest, and promote in order to demonstrate the productivity of schools of choice.

Saying, for example, that the virtuous cycle requires major investments in R&D is not to oppose the working of market forces. Such actions are what make a market, particularly in a government-dominated industry, start to work as theory would suggest it will. Strategy, problem-solving, and concerted action are not inimical to development of a market in education; they are necessary means to it. Strategy and concerted action are needed in six areas:

+ Funding Choice
+ Supporting Emergence of New Schools
+ Stimulating Innovation
+ Improving the Teacher Labor Force
+ Re-missioning States and School Districts for Continuous Improvement
+ Strengthening State Laws Governing Choice

Funding Choice

The immediate remedy for the problems in funding choice is a policy change that would ensure that charter or voucher schools receive as much money to educate children as do district-run public schools. Such measures, which could be written directly into charter and voucher laws, would allow new schools to compete effectively for teachers, principals, and other assets, and ensure that their instructional budgets were not drawn down by expenses that other publicly funded schools did not have to pay.

Those measures alone, however, would not be enough to fuel the virtuous cycle. Choice must also force equivalent movements of funds out of district-run schools when children transfer to charter or voucher schools. Otherwise, districts and the schools they run have little incentive to make competitive responses, which could in turn lead to innovation and experimentation with new forms of teaching and ways to use human resources. Thus, the virtuous cycle requires changes in the ways regular public schools are funded. [1]

Choice supporters might think their only concern is equal funding for charter schools and larger vouchers. They are wrong. Those measures could accelerate growth of the choice sector but that is only half of the equation. The core funding for district-run schools must be easy to move as students move. If districts can hide money in administrative accounts or protected programs, they can be insulated from the consequences of students moving to schools of choice. If all their money moves when students move (as is the case for charters and voucher schools), districts will be forced to compete for students. That will make the virtuous cycle real.

Public education is now financed in ways inimical to choice. Dollars will not flow in ways required for the virtuous cycle contained in Figure 1 until district funds management becomes pupil- rather than program-based and dollars flow with children to the schools they attend. There are proposals for such changes, both from those who would make school districts more transparent and efficient and from choice advocates. However, unions and district finance managers oppose proposed changes to state finance

1. For a complete exposition of these points, see Paul T. Hill, Marguerite Roza, and James Harvey, *Facing the Future: Financing Productive Schools* (Seattle, WA: Center on Reinventing Public Education, University of Washington, 2008).

laws and are working to block efforts to strengthen federal grant requirements that would require equal state and local spending on all students.

Most states now distribute money for K–12 education in ways that make particular uses of funds permanent. But those funds would, in a system built to exploit the virtuous cycle, be considered contingent on enrollment and therefore movable. This is so even when states fund things that schools certainly need. Washington and North Carolina, for example, tie most state funding to teacher slots, one teacher for approximately every 20 students. This cements one use of funds in place and makes it difficult for district-run schools to change or experiment with new ideas. What is to say that schools might not be more productive, at least for some children, by employing a different number of teachers than the state pays for, or by using some of the funds now dedicated to teachers to purchase online materials or instruction provided by museums or scientific institutions? The answer is, there is no evidence.

The same is true of fixed administrative structures. These is no evidence that schools employing less than the numbers of administrators funded under state school finance formulas are less productive. To the contrary, there is reason to think that schools could be more productive if they traded in some administrators so they could spend more money on teachers or technical resources.

Other fixed uses of funds are also counter-productive. For example, states want high school students to learn chemistry and biology but, given the many productive ways of integrating the two subjects into one superior course, there is no reason to fund instruction in a way that suggests these subjects should be taught separately. In fact there is every reason for states to distribute money in ways that are wide open to combining courses and making other uses of funds that no one has yet thought of. The only way Americans can ever know whether some uses of funds are more productive than others is to allow many different uses and to closely track and compare the results.

How can states provide money for K–12 education in ways that encourage the virtuous cycle? Not, as we have shown, by funding things whose value relative to plausible options is unproven. The answer is that states should fund something that is permanent, not contingent. Others might imagine different ways to do this but one way is obvious: states should tie money to the one element of the education system to which they should be unconditionally committed—to students. There is nothing else in the education system that should receive the protection of a fixed amount of funding regardless of its productivity or the existence of promising alternatives. In effect, any scheme that funds something other than students implicitly puts consequences for students second to the continuation of some program, administrative structure, or group of employees.

Tying money to students means allocating a specific amount for every child in the state and distributing money to districts and schools solely on the basis of enrollment. States could decide to allocate more for one group of children than for another (e.g., allocating more than the average amount of money to support education of children who do not speak English). But consistent with *not* funding things whose value is unknown, states would allocate money to states and districts for those children's education, rather than for any specific program or administrative structure.

If states would combine all the money they now spend on K–12 education, divide it up by enrollment, with the same fraction of the total assigned to each child, and distribute dollars to school districts and charter schools in the same way, they could simultaneously eliminate both the financial barriers to the virtuous cycle driven by choice, and the confusion about where state money goes. The virtuous cycle could move even faster if states were willing to experiment with greater amounts of money in some cases to see what it could buy, or with ways of combining money from education and social services for more comprehensive educational and social programs.

Tying money to students could encourage formation of new schools and expose existing schools to the financial consequences of competition. However, simple accounting changes would not be enough. State or local district officials could easily revert to old habits, controlling uses of funds centrally and only imputing budget allocations to students and schools. To drive the virtuous cycle, money must actually follow children and its use must be determined at the school level. Thus, districts would need to be able to demonstrate that actual spending on schools and groups of students reflected the allocations they received from the state.

A new funding system must also make sure that all funds move from one school to another as students transfer. This could be accomplished via a voucher or by a centralized accounting structure that transferred a set amount of money to a school for every day a student is enrolled. Free movement of funds would affect school budgets immediately, creating incentives for schools to avoid losing students to other schools.

Such movements of funds could hollow out some school districts so they are responsible for only a few schools. However, if school districts want to avoid being a school provider of last resort, serving only students whose parents are too naïve or overwhelmed to make decisions about their children's education, they will be driven by choice into managing all their schools on the basis of performance, eliminating ones no one wants to attend and constantly looking to build more attractive alternatives.

Thus, reaching the full potential of choice requires reform of the basic ways states fund schools. Proposals for such changes in state finance systems have recently emerged, first for California[2] and then for other states.[3] States are likely to move slowly toward student-based funding, but even incremental changes will help drive the virtuous cycle. Supporters of choice might be reluctant to get tangled up in questions about how district-run schools are funded, thinking these have nothing to do with the emergence and quality of charter and voucher schools. The opposite is true: basic school finance, as determined by state law and policy, will determine whether the positive effects of choice will be broad or narrow.

Federal legislation could also help promote student-based funding. As this is written there is a proposal to revive the "comparability" provision of the federal Title I program.[4] This provision, first introduced in the early 1970s, required school districts to demonstrate that schools receiving federal aid were not short-changed in the allocation of state and local funds. These provisions were turned into dead letters in the late 1970s, as localities were allowed to ignore school-to-school differences in teacher salaries and allocation of other resources. Once it was discovered that schools receiving Title I funds often received smaller shares of state and local funds than

2. Susanna Loeb, Anthony Bryk, and Eric Hanushek, *Getting Down to Facts: School Finance and Governance in California*, Stanford, Institute for Research on Education Policy, 2007.

3. The National Working Group on Funding Student Learning, *Funding Student Learning: How to Align Education Resources with Student Learning Goals*, Seattle, School Finance Redesign Project, 2008. See also Paul T. Hill, Marguerite Roza, and James Harvey, *Facing the Future: Financing Productive Schools* (Seattle,WA: Center on Reinventing Public Education, University of Washington, 2008).

4. See Phyllis McClure, Ross Wiener, and Marguerite Roza, Matt Hill, *Ensuring Equal Opportunity in Public Education: How Local School District Funding Practices Hurt Disadvantaged Students and What Federal Policy Can Do About It*, Washington, Center for American Progress, 2008.

other schools in the same districts, Rep. George Miller (D-California) proposed reviving the original comparability provisions.

These proposals would give school districts a number of years to re-allocate their funds. Rather than forcibly reassign teachers, districts could equalize spending incrementally as teachers retire, allocating only enough funds for a starting teacher salary to a school with above-average spending, and allocating the funds saved to schools with below-average spending.

Restoring Title I comparability rules would not by itself create the forms of mobile student-based funding needed to fuel the virtuous cycle. But doing so would be a move in the right direction, requiring districts to change their resource allocations so that per-pupil amounts could be readily computed and shown to be equal.

Supporting Emergence of New Schools

Funding levels and state charter caps are a strong constraint on the growth of new schools of choice. In 2007, with the exception of six states that are still below their caps (California, Florida, Ohio, Wisconsin, Maryland, and Texas), most states with charter schools opened five or fewer new schools. Eight states with charter school laws opened none.[5] Lifting of New York's charter cap in 2007 led to formation of eighteen new charter schools in 2008.

The numbers of private schools, and of independent schools redeeming government tuitions, have not grown appreciably for years. Clearly, political and legislative action on charter caps is an important precondition for growth of new schools.

Anticipating relaxation of caps, pro-charter philanthropies have worked for years on a strategy for "scaling up" chartering—increasing

5. Jon Christensen and Robin Lake, "The National Charter School Landscape in 2007," in Robin Lake, ed., *Hopes, Fears, and Reality: A Balanced Look at American Charter Schools in 2007* (Seattle, WA: Center on Reinventing Public Education, University of Washington, 2007).

the overall numbers of charter schools and the numbers of localities in which charter schools are operating. The preferred solution has been Charter Management Organizations. CMOs are nonprofit organizations that manage multiple charter schools. CMOs are like Education Management Organizations (EMOs) except that the latter are for-profit organizations.

In theory, CMOs and EMOs should make it easier to form schools of choice, both by reducing the administrative burdens on school leaders and by helping schools develop strong cultures, positive parent relations, and effective approaches to instruction. However, based on our previous studies it is clear that these organizations differ tremendously in what they do for member schools, the amount and quality of what is provided, and how much is spent on central functions. Among functions they perform are:

Performing market analysis before schools start
Handling political issues before schools start
Arranging facilities
Handling legal work
Assisting with human resources:
    Accounting, payroll, and benefits
    Marketing materials
    Leader selection and training
    Board selection and training
    Teacher selection and evaluation
    Teacher compensation and incentive systems
Providing instructional materials
Training teachers in use of materials
Training leaders and teachers in parent relations
Managing school start-up
Networking schools for mutual self-help

Assessing student progress

Intervening to resolve academic problems

Intervening when outcomes fail to improve via consulting, networking

Intervening to solve board and management problems

Despite the amounts of money invested in CMOs (approximately $150 million to date) there are questions about what CMOs add to the numbers and quality of charter schools. (This author is principal investigator on a major study of these topics.) CMO-run schools are still a small minority of charter schools, approximately 250 of nearly 4,000. If existing CMOs grow to the limits of their current plans they might together create a total of about 1,100 schools.

It is not yet clear whether CMO affiliated schools start up more smoothly, survive longer, or provide more effective instruction. It is clear that CMOs have cornered a great deal of the philanthropic money available to encourage new schools of choice, and that the schools they assist are less diverse than other charter schools. In some cases CMOs have been controlling enough that their affiliated schools barely meet the definition of a charter as an independently managed school.

Whatever the ultimate findings about CMOs, it is clear that they cannot be the full answer to the scaling problem. EMOs, with profit motives and greater access to business expertise, might be able to operate on a larger scale. But only a few, notably Edison and National Heritage Academies, have done so to date. Moreover, the political opposition to for-profit school providers is a significant barrier to increasing numbers of schools via EMOs. Even as EMOs and CMOs expand and multiply, it is important to facilitate the development of new independent schools of choice.

One organization, KIPP (Knowledge Is Power Program), is trying a franchising model, which does not require the kind of constant central management provided by CMOs and EMOs. Though franchising has its own problems of quality control, it might prove less costly and more expandable than CMOs and EMOs.

Simpler institutions like incubators that help schools open and then cut them loose might help increase the numbers of new schools. Existing CMOs might also assist schools for shorter lengths of time rather than maintaining oversight indefinitely.

As I will argue in the next section, CMOs and other scaling-up models like franchises could be far more effective if there were proven instructional systems that they could adopt and reproduce. A serious R&D enterprise could provide significant productivity advantages for schools of choice, accelerating their growth rate.

A totally different approach would be for philanthropies to sponsor formation of local service providers that would charge fees to help new schools with financing, insurance, legal representation, payroll, leasing, transportation, and student testing. Because school districts do most of these things internally, few communities have vendors equipped to do them effectively for charter schools.

Philanthropies and local charter associations might also create other community institutions that would together make life easier for schools of choice. These could include clearinghouses for parent information about charter school offerings, training centers where people who want to work in schools of choice could learn the special management and collaborative skills required, and registries where school heads could find teachers and principals who have experience in schools of choice. Philanthropies and local business groups could also create independent real estate trusts to develop and manage facilities for rent at low rates to schools of choice, and broker formation of risk pools through which schools of choice could jointly fund services for handicapped students.

The value of the latter approach is that it would focus on making whole communities more receptive environments for schools of choice. Rather than centralizing support in an organization that provides support for schools in many localities (e.g., a CMO), this approach would focus on supporting the whole charter sector in one locality. In localities where this was done, all schools of choice could benefit because families would be accustomed to exercising choice; information about schooling options would be easy to obtain; individual schools would have known track records and established clienteles; there would be a large supply of teachers who had worked in or attended schools of choice; the overall teacher supply would be good because new teachers and individuals with rare skills could compete for jobs and be paid for the value of their contribution to the school, not just for their seniority or degrees attained; and business and financial institutions would understand schools and compete to supply them with everything from loans and insurance to facilities, maintenance, and supplies.

Even with a combination of CMO, EMO, franchise and community readiness strategies, new schools will remain hard to start. Their growth rate will determine the pace at which choice fuels the virtuous cycle. As this is written, no one knows how fast that growth rate could be.

Stimulating Innovation

Today, there is no significant source of tested and proven technology applications for schools of choice to draw from. The absence of serious R&D has handicapped the charter movement, which can show only mixed emotions that it offers schools that will produce better results than regular public schools. Critics of the No Child Left Behind provisions requiring districts to consider charters as alternatives for children in failing schools score points when they claim that charter schools might not be any better. In general, the lack of proven methods, and of effective mixtures of teacher work, materials, and technologies that can be readily reproduced, are major deficits in the choice movement.

Parents of "mainstream" students would be much more likely to transfer to schools of choice if those schools could offer forms of instruction that lived within available budgets but were proven via clinical trials to be much more effective than those used in existing district-run schools. Such forms of instruction might combine disciplined teacher work with use of online instructional packages to teach subjects in which teachers are weak. They might also include detailed tracking of student progress on key skills and rapid adaptation of instruction in light of individual student results. Some might be highly unconventional (e.g., delivery of most instruction online with limited use of teachers as diagnosticians and tutors).

The lack of organized R&D on possible uses of technology limits innovation and slows down the virtuous cycle. This problem is not likely to be solved by entrepreneurship or informal tinkering. It almost certainly requires a formal R&D enterprise analogous to those that develop medical therapies or new defense systems that integrate human and machine work in order to accomplish new missions.

In fields such as medicine and defense, new technologies do not simply emerge through tinkering on the part of practitioners. In fact, most big advances come despite practitioners, who would rather not undergo the cost and inconvenience of changing their work. This is likely to be true in education as well. Charter school educators, like their counterparts in district-run schools, regard themselves as practitioners of an art and carriers of a moral tradition, not users of science. They are more likely to resent and resist new ideas about instruction than to welcome or seek to develop them.

In fields where innovation is constant, specialized institutions— Defense Advanced Research Projects Agency (DARPA) and National Institutes of Health (NIH)—organize R&D. Research and development intermediaries like DARPA and NIH exist for three reasons: because basic scientists and inventors do not have the financial resources or the operational knowledge to build their discoveries into complete systems; because risks are high and costly failures inevitable; and because the end users have little incentive to try something that disrupts their operating routines or threatens to make cherished skills obsolete. Intermediaries have the funds to assemble multiple emerging technologies into systems, develop the systems, subject them to rigorous proof, and press for adoption of those that accomplish needed new tasks or do existing tasks better.[6]

Parallels to education are strong. There are many inventors in education, from individual teachers to software companies developing small instructional and testing modules. Paul Allen's Apex Learning company has developed online Advanced Placement courses, but not programs for whole schools. The online vendor K–12 Inc. targets a niche market. Home-schoolers, entities seeking to serve school dropouts, and schools in remote areas have been open to heavy use of online instruction. But school districts have not been interested, except insofar as online instruction attracts children who might otherwise not attend school at all. Districts

6. Ben Rich's book *Skunk Works: A Personal Memoir of My Years at Lockheed* (New York: Back Bay Books, 1996) is particularly eloquent about resistance to new systems and the need for rigorous testing and demonstration to spur adoption.

adopt technology applications piecemeal, as add-ons to existing courses or for tutoring. School districts and unions resist any approach to instruction that would change the work of teachers or reduce the numbers needed.

Technology entrepreneurs, understanding that there is money to be made in providing what districts want to buy, stick to piecemeal programs or marginal situations. The results are familiar: unused computers and little change in regular classroom instruction, not efforts to integrate materials delivered via electronic means into core instructional plans.

Thus, in K–12 education innovative ideas exist but they are seldom assembled into instructional systems: plans for combining technology with student and teacher work in new ways, either for teaching an entire subject or for operating a whole school. Nor are innovations tested to the point that their effectiveness and best application can be considered proven. Moreover, there is no mechanism for moving new instructional systems into widespread use.

The virtuous cycle depends on innovation that is now blocked by practitioner resistance and low funding for schools of choice. A process for developing and proving instructional innovations is an essential driver of the virtuous cycle, whether by providing new schools with technical advantages or by giving existing schools ideas about how they can compete effectively.

In this environment, how can we move toward innovations that will produce more effective instructional systems and therefore give us real evidence about how much money is needed and how it should be used? Moving the whole public education system at once is too hard, and appealing to only the most innovation-minded teachers and administrators leads to short-term initiatives that are abandoned as soon as a key person retires or takes a new job. The key is to enter public education through the one part of it that has strong incentives to find and use performance-enhancing initiatives: charter schools.

The R&D initiative described above could give charter schools the ideas and methods they need to compete effectively. As multi-school providers, EMOs and CMOs would gain a tremendous advantage if they could adopt proven, reproducible methods. Foundations that sponsor R&D can promote adoption of proven ideas by building new EMOs and CMOs around proven methods.

Charter schools could also serve as sites for full field-testing of instructional systems proven in clinical trials. As in medicine, large-scale use of a system would reveal interactions and consequences too rare to be seen in controlled environments. As in defense, field trials would reveal the need for adjustments in training and support, and sharpen estimates of cost. A final stage of the R&D process, which an R&D intermediary must pay for, is close unbiased tracking of large-scale program implementation and student effects.

Government has pockets deep enough to pay for development and testing of many alternative systems, and to tolerate the inevitably high rate of failure. However, federal government efforts to create NIH-like entities in education (e.g., the National Institute of Education in the 1970s) have foundered on the same politics of competing certitudes that have rendered the public education system itself unable to improve. As this is written the U.S. Department of Education has announced a $650 million innovation fund that sets aside only $5 million for ideas that are not already in operation and can be validated via hard performance data. This fund is therefore highly unlikely to sponsor new instructional systems outside the boundaries of current practice.

An alternative—foundation funding for an R&D intermediary—is possible, especially with some extremely deep pockets, such as the Gates and Hewlett foundations have. However, these organizations too would need to keep hands off for a long time, accept frequent failures, and resist the temptation to mandate work on whatever is currently politically correct.

Improving the Teacher Labor Force

Though CMOs have been the main focus of efforts to increase the numbers of charter schools, the supply of teachers able and willing to work in schools of choice might be the most important constraint on scale. As we have seen, teachers from unique sources like Teach For America are important but small contributors to the charter school teaching force. Pro-choice philanthropies might consider greatly expanding Teach For America and The New Teacher Project, though it is far from clear that they could recruit enough new college graduates willing to postpone other career plans. There is only one reliable source of large numbers of teachers, and that is the group of people who have attended schools of education and are prepared to teach in conventional public schools. Though experienced public school teachers are problematic for schools of choice—too many have learned to like the job security and insulation from performance pressures that district employment offers— newly minted teachers are a promising source.

Despite the low average ability of new education school graduates,[7] education schools still produce significant numbers of capable graduates with decent subject-matter knowledge. This

7. See Eric A. Hanushek and Richard R. Pace, "Who Chooses to Teach (and Why)?" *Economics of Education Review*, 14(2), June, 1995, pp. 101-117. See also Hanushek and Pace, "Understanding Entry into the Teaching Profession," in Ronald G. Ehrenberg, ed., *Choices and Consequences: Contemporary Policy Issues in Education* (Ithaca, NY: ILR Press, 1994) pp. 12-28.

high-ability group is much more likely than other new teachers to dislike the working conditions in district-run schools and to leave teaching within the first few years.[8] New teachers are much less likely to support union demands,[9] more likely to want to teach in demanding locales, and more willing to sacrifice job security for challenge and satisfaction.

Some charter schools recruit young education school graduates, but they offer lower pay and worse benefits than do district-run schools, deals that many new college graduates can't accept. For charter schools to attract large numbers of the ablest education school graduates, they need to offer competitive pay and benefits. Their higher workloads and performance pressures can be an asset in recruiting young teachers, but charters need to offer a competitive short-term financial deal. Some young teachers who expect to move back and forth between teaching and other work throughout their careers might see a financial advantage in charter schools that offered fully vested portable pensions.

Filling teacher slots is one reason why charter schools need to attract graduates who might otherwise work in district-run schools. A second reason is to change the public school teaching force. Early experience in charter schools is likely to affect teachers throughout their careers, even if they eventually work in district-run schools. Over time, the numbers of certified teachers who

8. Eric Eide, Dan Goldhaber, and Dominic Brewer, "The Teacher Labour Market and Teacher Quality," *Oxford Review of Economic Policy*, 20, 2004, pp. 230-244. See also Goldhaber and Brewer, "Does Teacher Certification Matter? High School Teacher Certification Status and Student Achievement," *Educational Evaluation and Policy Analysis*, 22(2), 2000, pp. 129-145.

9. Dan Goldhaber, Scott DeBurgomaster, and Michael DeArmond, "Teacher Attitudes about Compensation Reform: Implications for Reform Implementation" (Seattle, WA: Center on Reinventing Public Education, University of Washington, 2007). See also Goldhaber and DeArmond, *A Leap of Faith: Redesigning Teacher Compensation*, Seattle, Center on Reinventing Public Education, 2008.

know what it means to work in a charter school, or who have colleagues with charter school experience, is likely to grow. Teachers for a New Era is working to change teaching forces in a number of big cities. But again, its output of teachers is low compared to the numbers of new teachers hired. There is no substitute for increasing the numbers of new teacher graduates who consider working in charter schools.

Today the teaching force in most school districts is insular and totally patterned by experience within a bureaucracy. However, turnover among district teachers is rapid enough—nearly 10 percent annually in many places—to allow a significant transformation in a few years. In the future it should be possible for charter schools to find large numbers of teachers in the place where most of the teachers are.

Aside from campaigning for financial parity between charters and district-run schools, choice supporters can do other things to help solve the charter school teaching force problem. One is to experiment with new technology-assisted teacher roles that could both reduce the numbers of teachers needed and make charter employment extremely attractive to the most imaginative teachers. A second is to study the human resource policies of charter schools that have learned how to succeed with only a few experienced teachers, and make the findings broadly available to CMOs and charter school boards.

State and local charter school associations could also greatly strengthen their relationships with colleges of education, to make sure able graduates know about the charter option. Individual charter schools make such connections, but state and local associations could work on behalf of all charter schools in their areas by offering presentations, on-campus interviews, and visits to charter schools. The same associations could also create registries of potential charter school teachers, including new graduates, former charter school teachers, and current private and parochial school teachers, through which individual schools can contact prospective teachers.

Changes in the K–12 teaching force are a critical element of the virtuous cycle, both because charter school growth depends on a supply of teachers and because greater numbers of district-employed teachers need to know what it means to work in a high-performing school. Efforts to create a special supply of teachers through Teach For America and The New Teacher Project are important, but they cannot do everything that is needed.

Re-missioning States and School Districts for Continuous Improvement

Unless existing public school districts are forced to seek the best possible ways to educate students and use funds, the virtuous cycle will be limited to a few zones of big cities or, at best, to a few large urban districts. On the other hand, if districts are required to provide the best possible opportunities for all their students, and to abandon any school or program in favor of one that is likely to be more productive, choice is likely to spread indefinitely.

Unfortunately, public education, at both the state and local levels, is not structured for adaptation. Resources are allocated to specific programs and functions and reallocation is deliberately made difficult. Employees are hired for the duration of their professional lives and jobs are not expected to change dramatically. Individual incomes are linked to longevity, not productivity or adaptability. Virtually all money is committed to current services and programs; there is little or nothing for new investments or rewards for performance or innovation. R&D investments are minuscule.

Pressure to change this is coming from the policy ferment about school choice; governors and legislators are learning that money is used in so many obviously unproductive ways that no one can say how much must be spent to educate all children effectively. For the first time, states and school districts are apparently open to proposals for funding schools in ways that are transparent, flexible, and accountable.

The new ideas gaining currency in public education reform come together under the term *continuous improvement*. Continuous improvement is an idea imported from business. Firms in competitive markets assume that their current products and methods of production are never perfect, and might soon prove inadequate, even if they are now better than ever before. Businesses that operate under these assumptions constantly seek to replace their own products with something that serves customers better, and replace their weakest products and operating units even if their performance isn't disastrously bad. An entity committed to continuous improvement:

Assumes that its current product line will soon become obsolete

Expects that competitors will find ways to deliver more for the same money

Rewards people who get ideas about improving and cutting the cost of producing current products and services

Invests in new ideas but, knowing that only a few will be worth pursuing, expects to abandon many

Expects ultimately to abandon or replace its current products and services, and tries to replace them faster and better than competitors can

Pursues higher performance any way it can, including by forming alliances with one-time competitors.

These ideas require changes in the ways states and localities fund K–12 education and in the missions and capacities of local school districts.

Funding continuous improvement: In the context of school finance, proposals for continuous improvement involve changing rules on the allocation and use of public funds so that these goals are realized:

+ Money and people can flow from approaches that are less productive to those that are more productive.
+ Potential innovators are encouraged to invest time and money developing new approaches.
+ Fair comparisons can be made between new and dominant approaches.

If the idea of continuous improvement were applied to K–12 public education, even a relatively high performing school, teacher, or instructional program would be assumed not to be the best possible. All arrangements, even those that look good at the present time, would be subject to challenge and replacement by something better.

Proposals for a school finance system based on continuous improvement would have states make three kinds of changes in law and policy, as summarized in Table 2.

As the second column of the table shows, to create a continuous improvement system state leaders would need to do more than make positive changes in their funding laws and regulatory structures. They would also need to eliminate statutory and regulatory provisions that hide uses of funds or tie up dollars for the support of institutions, programs, and employees whose productivity needs to be proven, not assumed. These changes are fundamental: all

Table 2: Principles and Steps toward Continuous Improvement in K–12

People and money flow from less to more productive uses	Fund students, not programs or adults Account for use of funds down to the school, classroom, and student Move money administratively or via choice
Alternative uses of funds are fairly compared	Link records on spending, services, student characteristics, and outcomes Compare programs, schools, teachers on a cost-effectiveness basis
Incentives for innovation	Encourage unprecedented uses of funds, methods, technologies, and human resources Maintain neutrality between conventional and new providers of schools, instruction

would require redesign of legislation, regulation, and state accounting systems.

The first steps toward continuous improvement are to adopt transparent pupil-based funding and eliminate arbitrary constraints on uses of money. If a significant amount of money is used for purposes whose effectiveness is not proven—for administrative units that exist now only because they have existed for a long time—potentially more effective uses of the same money are rendered impossible.

Table 2 does not answer a big question: should states allocate money to districts and let them make decisions about how to spend it, or require that districts pass money on to schools and let school leaders make spending decisions? The answer is that states could choose either course of action, as long as they require districts to account for funds down to the level of the student. With that requirement it would be clear how money was used and what individual students experienced.

Of course, allocating money directly to schools is likely to generate greater diversity in practice. This could lead to more innovation and to competition from schools other than those run by the district. Districts would be in a new business: obtaining the best schools they can from any mix of sources that can provide them. The next section discusses what this new role for districts entails, and why it promotes choice and continuous improvement.

Re-missioning school districts: Opening and closing schools is an essential part of the virtuous cycle. If these things don't happen—particularly if low-performing district-run schools are not closed and replaced with new higher-performing schools in significant numbers—the effects of choice are likely to be limited.

Milton Friedman's pure theory of school choice would rely on the market, not government, to determine which schools opened or closed. Under the U.S. legal system, however, it is impossible to see how courts and government agencies could take a completely hands-off approach to publicly funded education. Civil rights laws guaranteeing equal access to schools, health and safety regulations, and deeply established service guarantees for handicapped children would constrain schools' freedom and ultimately help determine which ones could stay open and receive public funds. It is also difficult to see how demands for student protection and accountability for public funds would not lead to a licensing regime that would ultimately put some government agency in charge of judging schools' fitness.

John Chubb and Terry Moe's seminal book, *Politics, Markets, and America's Schools,* acknowledged Friedman but made a far different proposal for school choice with significant government oversight. They showed how existing oversight mechanisms work against school quality but argued that much simpler forms of oversight would allow formation of better schools while maintaining civil rights protections and reasonable clarity about uses of public funds. Chubb and Moe proposed that government would license schools, preventing incompetent organizations from opening schools in the first place; government would also provide common information on school performance to inform parental choices. They assumed that a choice system could not survive egregious school actions—racial discrimination, financial abuses, and academic failure—and invented a modest governmental role. Chartering and school contracting are essentially variants on their licensing proposal.

Sensible though such ideas about limited governmental oversight look, they have been difficult to put into practice. Charter authorizers have struggled to make judgments about school quality and to decide what to do about a school that gets poor student results. School districts, required by No Child Left Behind to identify schools in need of major improvements and to provide options for children in low-performing schools, have fumbled the assignment.

Responsible public oversight of school performance is essential to the full operation of choice's virtuous cycle. Low-performing schools must be closed and students allowed to go to higher-performing schools, so that on average the quality of education will rise. New schools, either imitating existing effective schools or trying out promising ideas about instruction and student services, must be allowed to form, so that the quality of schools available in a community will continuously rise.

However, despite the existence of charter laws and the performance pressures created by No Child Left Behind, few local school districts have developed the capacity to track the performance of individual schools and decide which ones need help, which can be left alone, and which need to be closed so students can transfer to other schools where they have some chance of learning. Charter school authorizers—including universities, state agencies, nonprofit organizations and some school districts—have grappled with the oversight problem more seriously but they too are struggling with the big questions, especially about when to give up on a low-performing school and what to do for students in a school that must be closed.

A new study of performance-based management in other sectors reveals a great deal about how it can be done in education.[10] Organizations conducting performance-based oversight may delegate, but they never abandon, their responsibility for results. Leaders of businesses and government agencies can decide whether to rely on one provider or another, or on their own employees, to perform a particular task. But no matter to whom work is assigned, top leaders remain ultimately responsible for its being done. If one arrangement (e.g., relying on employees) does not get the needed results, top leaders must develop options.

One option always available is to leave the task in the same hands but to make changes—greater resources, more training, expert advisors, more capable employees—that make success more likely. However, performance managers are not free to abdicate responsibility by saying, "We have tried and tried but the people to whom we assigned the task just can't do it, so we can do no more." This means that the responsible party must always make sure it has an option.

Organizations built for performance management abandon a struggling provider that has tried hard but failed to improve. "We

10. Paul T. Hill and Robin J. Lake, *Performance Management in Portfolio School Districts* (Seattle, WA: Center on Reinventing Public Education, University of Washington, 2009).

followed your advice" or "we obeyed all the rules" are no protection against a performance manager who thinks he or she has a better option.

With the exception of a few localities that have committed themselves to using chartering as one way their districts provide schools, leaders of public education have not even tried to adopt the capacity for performance-based management. But it can be done: school performance is difficult to judge but not more so than performance in complex technical areas.

It is clear that for school districts to do performance oversight they must be re-designed around a new mission, and contrary missions (e.g., prescribing details of school organization and instruction, central control of hiring and use of funds) must be terminated. Like other organizations that maintain portfolios of different providers, school districts will need to employ professional staff members who know enough about schools to identify promise and trouble, but who understand they can neither fix every problem they see nor insulate teachers and principals from the consequences of low performance. Such people will have to be developed over time; today, no one is trained for this job.

District performance oversight organizations must also be built on premises that are now foreign to school districts, including neutrality about who runs a school (district employees, nonprofits, for-profits) and clear accountability—only performance matters. Overseers must be willing to arrange help for a school but also to abandon it if it does not improve, recognizing that school closings are inevitable and desirable. They must understand that all choices are relative—it is easier to close a weak school if the alternative is known—and determine to open options by investing in new providers and seeking providers elsewhere.

Localities that have seized upon No Child Left Behind as a warrant to make their districts less tolerant of low performance (e.g., New York, Chicago, and the District of Columbia) have adopted forms of student-based funding, school-level control of hiring and spending, open enrollment, and performance-based decisions about whether to sustain or close schools. These districts (plus Hartford and Oakland) have also expressly used chartering as an element of their district transformation strategies.

If choice is ever to lead to full operation of the virtuous cycle, such changes in district policy must be much more widespread. Pro-choice scholars and philanthropists cannot afford to stay on the sidelines as localities try to transform their school districts, saying, "This is not our fight."

K–12 education is too frozen by politics, regulation, privilege, and contracts to reform itself without choice. However, those attributes of the conventional public education system also limit the effects of choice. There are things choice supporters can do to strengthen voucher and charter programs. But it does not make sense to regard state and local public education systems simply as rivals to be beaten or ignored. If school choice is to reach its full potential it will be both as a goad to and a beneficiary of changes in the way states and localities fund, authorize, and oversee all publicly funded schools.

Strengthening State Laws Governing Choice

Earlier Koret Task Force publications have identified the key policy changes that must be made and suggested political strategies that could accomplish them. Our book *Charter Schools Against the Odds* (2006) called for seven changes in state charter school policies:

+ Lift or eliminate caps on numbers of charter schools.
+ Equalize funding for students in charter and traditional public schools.
+ Create multiple authorizers and hold all authorizers accountable for the performance of the schools they oversee.
+ Provide direct state funding for authorizers.
+ Treat nonprofit and for-profit organizations equally in terms of their eligibility to operate public schools, funding, and performance accountability.
+ Allow multiple schools under one charter.
+ Eliminate fixed terms, and instead make continuation contingent on performance.

This list of recommendations is as sound now as it was more than three years ago. Some states have made progress on lifting charter caps, and U.S. Education Secretary Arne Duncan is pressing all states to increase the numbers of charter schools as a condition of receiving Race to the Top funds. A few states are working to clarify the duties of authorizers, and (as we will see below) some school districts are becoming competent authorizers. However, the foregoing list is still a very good guide to strengthening state charter laws.

Conclusion

Choice is a simple-sounding intervention. But if it is to transform public education as thoroughly as supporters hope, choice must set off a complex set of events that we have called the virtuous cycle. Choice can be defined as allowing parents to choose schools and providers to control their own approaches to instruction. But a system of choice involves much more than that.

Philanthropists, scholars, and policymakers can do a great deal—much more than they have done to date—to make it possible for choice to have all of its potentially good effects. Philanthropies can invest in new schools, richer local support environments, new routes into teaching, and new career structures for teachers. Policymakers can eliminate financial advantages enjoyed by one set of schools (those run by districts) over another (charters and other schools of choice) by tying public funds to students. Public officials can also change the legally defined missions and powers of school districts so that they can manage all their schools on the basis of performance, thus allowing weak schools to die and new options to emerge. Together, public officials and philanthropies can invest in building capacities for performance-based oversight by school districts and charter authorizers.

Taken together, these actions will make it much more likely that the virtuous cycle will start working in earnest. How long will it take to produce results, especially for children now in bad schools? The honest answer is that we do not know. But the results will come much earlier if the investments and policy changes described above are made.

We do know, however, that for choice to have its full potential effect on K–12 education, choice supporters need to broaden their agendas to include reform of state school finance systems and re-missioning of school districts.

The suggested broadening of the pro-school choice agenda will be challenging. But it can bring important rewards, possibly including a larger coalition seeking pro-choice policies. Most importantly, a broader pro-choice agenda can accelerate the virtuous cycle described in this book, in ways that a single-minded focus on choice alone cannot accomplish.

ABOUT THE AUTHOR

Koret Task Force member **Paul T. Hill** is the John and Marguerite Corbally Professor at the University of Washington Bothell. He directs the Center on Reinventing Public Education, which studies alternative governance, financing, human resources, and accountability systems for public elementary and secondary education.

Hill's recent work has focused on the reform of public elementary and secondary education, the reform of school finance, and school choice. He edited two earlier volumes for the Koret Task Force, *Choice with Equity* and *Charter Schools against the Odds*. Hill also chaired Brookings' National Working Commission on Choice in K–12 Education and authored its report, *School Choice: Doing It the Right Way Makes a Difference*. Among his other books are *It Takes a City: Getting Serious about Urban School Reform* and *Fixing Urban Schools*, both of which are to serve as resources for mayors and community leaders facing the need to transform failing big-city school systems.

Before founding the Center on Reinventing Public Education, Hill worked for seventeen years as a senior social scientist at RAND, where he served as director of Washington operations and director of the Education and Human Resources Program. As a government employee (1970–77) he directed the National

Institute of Education's Compensatory Education Study (a congressionally mandated assessment of federal aid to elementary and secondary education). He also served two years as a congressional fellow and a congressional staff member.

He holds a PhD and MA from Ohio State University and a BA from Seattle University, all in political science.

Hill lives in Seattle with his wife, Alice.

INDEX

EDUCATION
next
B O O K S

EDUCATION NEXT BOOKS address major subjects related to efforts to reform American public education. This imprint features assessments and monographs by Hoover Institution fellows (including members of the Hoover Institution's Koret Task Force on K–12 Education), as well as those of outside experts.

Advance Praise for
Learning as We Go: Why School Choice Is Worth the Wait

"*Learning as We Go* tells it straight. We can't get effective schools for kids who are not learning now without choice and competition. But to get what choice can deliver, we must give it a chance. That means serious changes in state policy, real investments in new methods, and honest information for parents who want to find the right schools for their children."

— **Howard Fuller**, founder, Black Alliance for Educational Options

"Paul Hill's *Learning as We Go* provides a thoughtful, balanced, and powerful analysis of choice-focused education reforms. A refreshing contrast to the stridency and absolutism of much of the school choice debate, it's essential reading for anyone concerned about improving American education."

— **Andrew J. Rotherham**, cofounder and publisher, *Education Sector*, and author of Eduwonk.com

"*Learning as We Go* is a concise but convincing argument about why we should not give up on the promise of charter schools, even if they have not yet substantially transformed our American education system. Hill deftly assesses the political, financial, and cultural barriers charter schools have faced and demonstrates effectively how each can be overcome, with better outcomes for students. You may not always agree with Hill, but this is a discussion well worth having."

— **Paul Teske**, dean of the School of Public Affairs and Distinguished Professor at the University of Colorado, Denver

"Hill clearly describes the choice debate and the need to balance the advantages of choice with other considerations and strategies to achieve systematic progress. As our experience has taught us in Louisiana, implementing choice alone is not enough. To make choice work, we must determine when and where choice models are more effective. We must also adopt policies and commit the necessary resources to ensure choice programs are poised for success. And we must attract new talent into our schools."

— **Paul G. Pastorek**, Superintendent of Education for the state of Louisiana